JESUS CEN

JESUS CENTRE STAGE

Theatre Radio Church Television

TONY JASPER
&
KENNETH PICKERING

Highland Books

Highland Books Ltd, Godalming, Surrey

First published in 2010 by Highland Books Ltd,
2 High Pines, Knoll Road, Godalming, GU7 2EP

ISBN: 978-1897913-87-1
ISBN-10: 1-897913-87-7

Printed in the United Kingdom
by CPI Mackays, Chatham

Contents

DEDICATION

Tony Jasper dedicates this book to Sandra Butterworth, Alan and Annette Smith for their constant practical concern during his illness in 2010, and to the friendship of Jon and Betty Dean.

THANKS TO Charlotte Emmett for help with the MS.

AUTHORS' NOTE

This book is the result of the collaboration between two writers with extensive and practical experience of theatre and the study of drama, theology and popular culture in the general arts field. They write as members of Christian churches and from a background of involvement with the presentation of Christian ideas through performance.

Although the book has involved constant discussion and debate between its two authors the first three chapters are essentially the work of Kenneth Pickering and the remaining chapters are by Tony Jasper. The final chapter brings the two authors together.

CHAPTER ONE

Enter Jesus

During the writing of this book the English National Opera Company announced that it would be performing Handel's *Messiah*, a choral work entirely focussed on the figure of Jesus, for two weeks in one of the largest theatres in London. This may have come as a surprise to many people for, surely, the *Messiah* is a national treasure that belongs securely to large choirs in churches and concert halls? Could it be that, on the brink of a new decade, the place to celebrate and think about the birth, life, death and resurrection of Jesus, was the theatre? Nobody ever mentions poor Jennings who compiled and selected the words, but Handel, who wrote the music of *Messiah* was, in fact, a man of the theatre and the work's first performance was in a theatre in Dublin. However, by that time, Handel had abandoned writing fashionable Italian Opera in favour of Oratorios that did not, in the usual sense require 'staging'. So the idea that *Messiah* should be 'staged' in the twenty-first century might seem even more surprising.

Of course, the term 'theatre' has several meanings. Theatre is not only a place, it is an art form, an activity and, for some, even a way of life. So perhaps we might rephrase my earlier question. Has the *way* to celebrate and think about the birth, life, death and resurrection of Jesus become 'theatre'? And theatre historians might add 'once again'.

Almost simultaneously with the announcement of the performances of *Messiah* the website of an organisation devoted to large-scale dramatic productions of the life of Jesus advertised the fact that they had obtained permission to stage a Passion Play in London's Trafalgar Square at Easter. It would seem that Jesus had, indeed, come centre stage and was experiencing high-profile exposure through the medium of theatre.

The Christian churches of various denominations have been somewhat suspicious of and sometimes downright hostile to the entertainment media. I well recall my Strict Baptist grandmother purchasing one of the few early television sets but insisting that it had doors which could be discretely closed 'when the Minister visited'. But even twenty years ago the parish priest of Oberammergau was saying of the famous Passion Play that it was 'inappropriate to call it "theatre", apparently oblivious to the huge package deals that brought audiences from all over the world to see the performances. We might ask if the thousands of dolls representing the baby Jesus seen in nativity plays every year are an aspect of 'theatre' or if they are somehow exempt from the opprobrium with which actors 'playing' Christ are sometimes viewed by Christians. Is Christ's childhood somehow less sacred than His manhood, perhaps? The answers may lie in new attitudes and a greater understanding of the nature of theatre as a fundamental human activity that will survive any intended repression and suppression. I recently heard an elder in the United Reformed Church explaining her experience in attending a series of sessions designed to enable certain nominated elders to be allowed to celebrate Holy Communion. When she expressed a feeling of inadequacy her tutor had said 'you are really an actor playing the part of Jesus'. For some this may seem almost blasphemous, for others it may help to explain why the Communion and dramatic re-enactment have such close links and why 'theatre' as we know it in the West, is often said to have originated in the Easter Mass.

The recent emergence of a website devoted to encouraging communities to stage their own Passion Plays and to use theatre as a form of witness whilst preserving high, professional standards of production, may be further evidence that old prejudices are breaking down. For what does the new generation of media-savvy Evangelical and charismatic Christians who choose to worship in sports halls, school halls and cinemas really know or care about the history of censorious attitudes of the churches that they have left half empty?

Very little I suspect. The new generation will use whatever communication medium fits its purpose, and this will include dance, acting, clowning, puppets, music, film, radio or digital technology.

However, many of the plays and theatrical events described in this book will have taken place against a background of some hostility and resistance from Christians and it is as well to confront this topic before we can go further.

In Britain the theatre still lives in the aftermath of two significant events although these are now distant in history. The first was the suppression of the 'Mystery Plays', a popular form of drama showing the whole story of Jesus, at some time in the sixteenth century. We do not know the precise reasons for this hostility to the plays but it is likely that it was the result of Puritan influence as part of the Protestant Reformation. The second more precise event was the closure of all theatres by the Puritan government of Oliver Cromwell at the time of the 'Commonwealth' in the seventeenth century. Even though this period of closure was no more than eleven years its legacy was long-lasting and the reopening of theatres at the time of the Restoration of Charles II was accompanied by much tighter controls.

So, given that many contemporary Christians are the successors of the Non-Conformists who brought about a change in attitudes to the theatre and that the Roman Catholic Church in Britain was equally slow in looking favourably on that art form we need to ask why the theatre was seen and possibly still is, as so undesirable. I would suggest that there are three main reasons: the first is that the theatre can be seen as being associated with riotous assembly and immoral living; the second that the theatre is essentially subversive and, thirdly, that there are particular objections to the representation of Jesus or any aspect of the deity on stage.

There is little doubt that, before the time of Cromwell, the theatre was a popular public meeting place where business deals, plots, assignations and discontent might well have been a natural part of the activity. It was obvious, therefore, that any authoritarian regime would see the theatre as a possible threat. If the theatre also provided an area for sexual infidelity and, indeed, may have encouraged it by its subject matter, it became an obvious target for Puritan objections. Even when the theatres re-opened after their enforced period of closure clergymen and laymen alike continued to thunder their disapproval in sermons, tracts and other broadsides. Their intensity was stoked by the first appearances of women on the English stage and many plays were condemned as showing and encouraging a decadent and immoral life-style. Defenders of drama then, as defenders of television and film now, would argue that the theatre's job was to show life as it is not as some clergyman would wish it. Christian suspicions have also focussed on the off-stage lives of many of theatre's practitioners, suggesting that they were dangerously 'bohemian' and, in Victorian times, this was exemplified by the fact that it was actresses who first advocated not wearing corsets! Such was the prejudice with which the nineteenth-century Church viewed theatrical performers that several bishops refused to give them communion and, for the Non-Conformist the theatre was a highly suspect territory. Ironically, the Non-conformists failed to notice the innate theatricality of their preaching and modes of worship. The popular Baptist preacher, Charles Haddon Spurgeon employed histrionic techniques to rival any Victorian actor and, later, the great Methodist preacher Dr. Sangster choreographed his own preaching moves before the mirror on a Saturday night. The mainstream revivalists all had a particular style - some were visual in their images for they conjured up for their congregation flames of fire and eternal damnation. Young men attempted to adopt the style of their favourite preachers, from gesture to voice modulation. I well remember my mother speaking in reverential terms of the way in which a particular minister entered from the vestry at the beginning of the service producing a hush of expectancy and 'working' his audience with as much skill as a great actor.

But the state had seemed to confirm the view of the churches for, in the eyes of the law, 'players' remained classified with 'rogues and vagabonds' for many years.

The theatre has not only hit back at many of these strictures by pointing out the relevance and deep seriousness of much of its work but also by the emergence of groups of

Christian actors, directors, dancers, technicians and designers who support the industry from the inside.

Pioneers and attitudes

Present day theatre practitioners who are able to stage aspects of the life of Jesus owe a great deal to the pioneering work of a number of almost legendary figures of the late nineteenth and early twentieth-century theatre. These include Sir Henry Irving, the first British actor to be knighted and thus bring a sense of respectability to his profession. Irving's most famous role in the closing years of his career was that of Thomas Becket, the Archbishop of Canterbury, in Tennyson's play *Becket* and all who saw the performance claimed it as a deep experience of faith. Irving had confronted the bigotry of the clergy in a famous address telling them to 'change their attitude' and assuring them that the theatre would join them in promoting more wholesome ways of living. Lilian Baylis, the remarkable manager of the Old Vic and later Sadler's Wells theatres brought the classic theatre and Shakespeare in particular to a new audience of low income enthusiasts and ran her theatre on a combination of flair, frugality and prayer. Convinced that she was doing God's will, she was instrumental in launching the careers of Sir Laurence Olivier and Sir John Gielgud and, like Irving, argued that the theatre was an educative medium that enriched and strengthened the moral life of the nation. Her producer, Harcourt Williams, who advocated a revolutionary manner of directing and performing Shakespeare, was also a devout Christian and was later to appear in central roles in the plays of one of the foremost Christian writers, Dorothy L. Sayers.

Irving, nevertheless, always maintained that the major achievement in reducing the hostility of the churches in the late nineteenth and early twentieth centuries lay with the Rev. Stuart Headlam, an Anglican curate who risked the disapproval of his bishop and jeopardised his chances of promotion by encouraging his congregation to read plays and attend the theatre. He is sympathetically portrayed in a thinly veiled disguise as the Rev. James Mavor Morell in George Bernard Shaw's play *Candida* and his name is still preserved in a trust he established to enable London school-children to see plays by Shakespeare. Headlam was convinced that the theatre could contribute to personal and community development in a unique way and was instrumental in helping to create the Actors' Church Union which not only continues to minister to the needs of actors but also acted as a forerunner to such organisations as the Arts Centre Group, Christians in Entertainment and Artisan, all of which now provide a forum for support and discussion of the arts as a facet of Christian life.

However, the suggestion that the theatre deals with issues central to human lives has often been seen by the Church as threatening and subversive. It is no co-incidence that tyrannical regimes always fear and suppress the theatres when they take power. The apartheid regime of South Africa was undermined by an organised 'theatre of protest' and Iranian playwrights now work in perilous conditions. The Church has always suspected that it is the theatre's task to pose difficult questions, to challenge authority, to interrogate the morality of policies, to put people's beliefs under the microscope and, as Shakespeare put it 'to hold the mirror up to Nature'. This can all be an uncomfortable business for an organisation like the Church that seeks to teach people what they should believe and what authorities to venerate. Unfortunately for much of its history the Church has sought to control and it has been perfectly comfortable with theatre as a means of this control. However, the moment that the Church has felt that it has lost control of the theatre it has become unhappy and hostile.

One of the most interesting debates in an area now known as 'performance studies' is the debate concerning what is collectively termed 'Carnival'. Such an activity would be seen as growing out of a community and might include celebratory processions, parades, carnival floats or similar forms of spectacle. Such events may well celebrate ethnicity or sexual orientation, local pride, history or trade and would certainly embrace the many processions and rituals associated with Easter in Catholic countries. Some scholars have argued that 'carnival' is an expression of people-power, of vibrant community and of shared beliefs and values. Others, however, have argued with equal conviction that carnival is simply another example of the status quo maintaining power by providing a safety-valve of apparent self expression whilst continuing to exercise control. This might well be said of those Catholic plays and pageants that dominate the lives of many communities at Easter but remain tightly under the control of the Church.

In Britain, the theatre has also been subject to various forms of state control and this has profoundly affected the way in which it has attempted to explore the Christian faith in an imaginative and honest way. With the 'Restoration' of the monarchy in 1660, King Charles II (who had spent a period of exile in the French court with its entertaining drama) was determined to re-establish the theatre, particularly as a part of the Court circle. Keenly aware of the theatre's ability to satirise and make political statements, Charles ordered his Master of the Revels, who was responsible for the licensing of all forms of public entertainment, to grant royal patents, establishing a monopoly on theatrical production in London to William Davenant and Thomas Killigrew.

Killigrew established himself at what became known as the Theatre Royal, in Drury Lane and his company was considered to be part of the Royal household. Davenant's patent eventually led to the establishment of the Theatre Royal, Covent Garden (now the Royal Opera House). This monopoly on the ability to produce 'legitimate drama' was reinforced by the Theatre Act of 1737. Play performances by touring companies could obtain a licence but were subject to strict control, however, some theatres and companies found ingenious ways of circumventing the Act by presenting what we can now see as the roots of 'Variety' and 'Musical Theatre'.

During the late eighteenth century royal patents were gradually granted to theatres in provincial towns and cities: Norwich; York; Hull; Liverpool; Newcastle; Manchester and Margate were among those to have their Theatre Royal. A further Act of law passed in 1788 legalised acting in the provinces by enabling local justices to grant licences to players for sixty days at a time and the 1843 Act for Regulating Theatres finally ended the monopoly of the theatres with a royal patent to produce 'legitimate drama'. All this activity greatly encouraged the building of theatres, many of which were named 'Theatre Royal' as a generic title rather than having any connection with royalty.

Censorship

The role of the Master of the Revels was eventually changed in title to 'Lord Chamberlain' and in this capacity he continued to exercise control and censorship over what could be performed in public until his office was abolished in 1968. Enshrined in the law which he was able to invoke were three forbidden ingredients for a stage play; nudity, obscene language and the representation of the deity. This final forbidden fruit provided a major stumbling block to those dramatists anxious to present aspects of the life of Jesus in dramatic form. When it came to considering plays submitted to him for licensing that contained 'religious' content the Lord Chamberlain invariably turned to the Archbishop of Canterbury for advice and usually found His Grace supportive of a refusal. Until 1913 there had been a total ban on any stage play dealing with biblical subjects but there had been increasing pressure from playwrights and producers for reversal of this position. Accordingly a number of biblical pageants and plays had been allowed to go ahead but the question of acting Jesus remained highly contentious. When in 1924, for example, the Archbishop, Randall Davidson was sent a play entitled *Judas Iscariot* he wrote to the Lord Chamberlain 'I wish they did not write these plays!' However, he did go on to say that, had the play been written by a well-known playwright such as George Bernard Shaw, he would have found the decision more difficult.

As it happened the Archbishop's fears were partly realised for in the same year no less a figure than the famous Christian poet, John Masefield submitted a play *The Trial of Jesus* which necessitated an actor to play the part of Jesus. This clearly exercised the Archbishop as he sensed Christian playwrights pushing at the boundaries of possibility and he conceded that the play had been written with great reverence and scriptural accuracy. But he finally pronounced to the Lord Chamberlain:

'I do not think protest would be awakened by the definite ruling that the Figure of our Blessed Lord Himself must not be produced in any drama which you sanction'.

Such is the early twentieth-century legacy of the theatre in Britain and the fight against it has exhausted and preoccupied many a playwright, actor and producer. Archbishop Davidson did not live to see a new and progressive Dean commission a play by Masefield for performance in his own Cathedral at Canterbury only four years after his 'definite ruling' and the play included the character of the 'Anima Christi'. Admittedly this was only the spirit of Christ before His birth but the revolution had begun!

A new world

In fact, Christian writers of the 1920s and 30s established a platform which produced some of the most influential and enduring religious literature and drama, but it was created at a time of crisis in belief. Such writers were filled with sheer horror at the man-made hell of the First World War. They had read the disturbing poetry of Sassoon and Brooke; the alarming lines of Wilfred Owen, "And Abraham arose and slew his son/ And half the seed of Europe, one by one" the ghastly statistics and details in Robert Graves' *Goodbye to All That*. They had seen R.C. Sherriff's memorable play about trench warfare *Journey's End* and terrifying images from painters and photographers; they heard dissonant music that challenged any concept of form or harmony. They had suffered personal loss and seen communities decimated by loss; they had witnessed a new role and independence for women; a refusal to return to old ways of servitude and deference. They had seen industrial unrest and unemployment; a frothy attempt by the bored affluent to party their way to happiness and, above all, they had experienced the collapse of simple faith and a growing sense that Christianity had little to say to this new waste land in the face of ever-intensifying materialism. There were also alarming shadows on the horizon of Europe.

Was it possible to catch a glimpse of God in such a situation? A group of writers that included J.R. Tolkein, Charles Williams and Dorothy L. Sayers thought that is was. Indeed, they called themselves 'the inklings' because they felt that they had an inkling of the nature and relevance of God. They, along with C.S. Lewis and T.S. Eliot found aspects of what they were seeking in allegory and in the ritual and liturgy of the High Church. Tolkein, an expert in ancient literature, produced his massive *Lord of the Rings* a complex allegory of the eternal battle between good and evil; Williams, a publisher and theologian, wrote a play about Thomas Cranmer, the Archbishop of Canterbury who had created the sublime words of the *Book of Common Prayer* but who eventually was burned for his adherence to principle; Dorothy L. Sayers, an Italian scholar made a verse translation of Dante's epic poem *The Divine Comedy* as well as writing a number of plays and C.S. Lewis is now best remembered for his remarkable Christian allegory *The Chronicles of Narnia* and through the play *Shadowlands*.

Modern readers or students of drama are more likely to be aware of T.S. Eliot's famous play *Murder in the Cathedral,* initially written, as were plays by Masefield and D.L. Sayers, for performance in Canterbury Cathedral. Almost alone amongst plays exploring aspects of the Christian faith produced during the 20s and 30s, this play broke into the London theatre scene and eventually established itself world-wide as a major classic. Its central figure, as with an earlier play by Tennyson that brought particular fame to Henry Irving, is Thomas Becket, the Archbishop who was murdered in his own cathedral. Like Jesus, Becket contemplates his approaching death and prepares his flock for the event through a memorable sermon. Patiently, Becket faces execution and explains to his perplexed followers that his death will not be without significance and that it is his destiny to die for a higher cause. Thus Eliot, who had created in his great poem *The Waste Land* an image of a world without meaning and hope, had provided in his play a sense that an individual, inspired by God, could make sense of existence and even experience peace beyond understanding.

The late 1920s and early 1930s saw a growing realisation among Christians that drama could be both a powerful medium for the exploration of faith and for evangelism. This resulted in the founding of the Religious Drama Society of Great Britain by a Non-Conformist, Olive Stephenson and Frances Younghusband in 1928. This society, which rapidly became known as Radius, has continued to promote high standards of Christian performance and writing through maintaining play collections and offering guidance in summer schools. Its first president was George Bell, who probably contributed more to the idea of a new and exploratory Christian drama than any other individual. He was Dean of Canterbury when he commissioned Masefield to write *The Coming of Christ* but then became Bishop of Chichester, in which role he continued to support a network of new playwrights and theatre practitioners and became celebrated for his opposition to the policy of obliteration bombing in the Second World War and his friendship and correspondence with the theologian Dietrich Bonhoeffer. Significantly, his final speech in the Convocation concerned the Church and the theatre.

The emergence of a specifically 'religious' drama in a predominantly secular Britain was largely a product of the traditionally strong amateur theatre movement together with a determination to include drama as an aspect of worship in some of the more progressive churches. This, however, carried with it the danger of worthy, pious and inadequately performed work which was not refined in the considerable heat of the professional theatre. It was this possibility of 'amateurish' writing and performance that preoccupied the founders of Radius and particularly its president, George Bell and his successor E. Martin Browne.

Whereas Bishop Bell was the source of inspiration to writers who aspired to explore aspects of Christianity in their plays it was the remarkable theologian-turned- theatre -director, E. Martin Browne who acted as midwife to their work and enabled a new generation of playwrights to shape their ideas into practical reality. Browne directed the plays of T.S. Eliot and Charles Williams and was also instrumental in encouraging Christopher Fry who ultimately became the most commercially successful of English Christian drama-tists in the immediate post-war years. Browne had showed himself to be a strict disciplinarian in rehearsals and, (conse-quently many would argue) able to achieve impressive results in a short time with both professional and amateur actors. He was also adept at exploiting what would now be labelled 'found spaces' and was able to mount plays in churches, ruins, halls and venues of all descriptions with flair and imagination. This skill became particularly relevant when, at the outbreak war in 1939, he and his actress wife, Henzie Raeburn, set up a professional touring company which travelled from its base in Canterbury to all parts of Britain staging Christian drama in whatever space they could find. Their search for suitable material was governed by a determination that it would be of the highest quality and included Eliot's *Murder in the Cathedral*. Two of their plays were based on biblical sources: James Bridie's *Tobias and the Angel* and D.H. Lawrence's *David* but when they wanted a suitable play for the Christmas season they turned to the Medieval Mystery plays and made their own compila-tion for these ancient sources. However, in seeking a play for Passiontide the company decided upon Henri Gheon's *The Way of the Cross* which not only caught the sombre mood of the war years but furthered the need for presenting inci-dents from the life of Jesus in dramatic form. The perfor-mance, which took place in such 'theatres' as miners' welfare clubs, schools and village halls, showed the events of the Judgement, Crucifixion and Resurrection of Jesus through the eyes of a narrator together with two men and two women who play out the scenes. A critic captured the essence of the play by saying of the actors: "they are spectators who are, as it were, outside time and space, who suddenly change into a tragic embodiment of the things they see". Jesus Himself does not appear in the play, instead, the action is conveyed by the stare or stamped foot by one of the actors.

Browne and his company argued that if people would not come to the theatre, then the theatre would come to them. This sense of energy has permeated much Christian drama and is evident today in the resurgence of new and original community plays, often taking the 'Passion' as their starting-point. E. Martin Browne remained a towering figure in the field of religious drama. His work was recognised by the award of a rare Lambeth Doctorate by the Archbishop of Canterbury and he was a pioneer director of the York Mystery plays as well as inaugurating the Program in Religious Drama at New York Theological Seminary (where one of his students would eventually write *Godspell*). Throughout his long career he had an obsession with high artistic standards and once famously remarked that 'much pious drama is impious art'. The story of the touring company which he and his wife ran during the war is engagingly told in their book *Pilgrim Story*(1945) but one wonders if the rapt audiences of schoolchildren pictured there as watching and listening to Eliot's *Murder in the Cathedral* were simply glad to be seeing live entertainment or enjoying a break from the routine of learning in difficult school conditions. Browne, like others who followed him may have labelled themselves too specifically as 'religious' drama specialists and eventually confined themselves too much to ecclesiastical buildings to make a substantial inroad into the thoughts of the vast majority of the population of post-war Britain.

However, in the 1920s and 30s, faced with the erosion of belief and the inadequacy of much Church life in the context of 'modern' attitudes, many Christian thinkers began to focus not so much on the distant and transcendental God but on the God who entered the torn world in human form. The upsurge of this 'Incarnational Theology' led to a renewed interest in the person, life and significance of Jesus, particularly among creative artists and, thus, for playwrights, the continuing prohibition of showing Jesus as a man and a character in a drama was a source of frustration and revolt.

The opportunity to challenge this entire aspect of censorship came when Dorothy L. Sayers committed herself to writing a radio play about the life of Christ to be broadcast during the Second World War. This play and its reception will be discussed in some detail in our chapter on the media but it is important to note here that the idea of Christ being impersonated by a human actor was seen by many conservative Christians as blasphemous and unacceptable. Interestingly, the actor in question was Robert Speight, who had played Thomas Becket in *Murder in the Cathedral*.

Playing Jesus

The problem of showing the person of Jesus in drama did not appear to concern the writers and performers of the many ancient Passion Plays that appear to have had their origins in the Middle Ages but Robert Potter, who has researched the revival of such plays in modern times argues in his book *The English Morality Play* (1975) that, for medieval actors, it was not a matter of 'representation' but a matter of 'presentation'. Those actors, he maintains, in no way claimed to represent or impersonate the figure of Jesus, they simply spoke the words and carried out the actions as a presentation. They did not 'inhabit the role' as a modern actor would put it or identify with the character they were playing. In practical terms this is a subtle distinction.

Both the contemporary theatre and broadcast media appear to be almost obsessed by 'realism'. We expect our characters to be believable and like other people we know; we are sometimes not sure if we wish to see actors in dramatic situations or 'real' people in 'reality' shows. If our stage and screen actors play parts we demand that they bring psychological and physical realism to their work and so, that is how they are trained. We expect to care about, relate to and love or hate our fictional people. We may well know more about them than we do about world leaders and we expect to share their lives.

When we go to see a play or film about Jesus we may well expect to feel the same. The actor must convince us that he is Jesus, and in many cases, *our* Jesus. Convinced that the most significant event in history is the entry of God in the form of a man early twentieth-century Christian dramatists argued that, far from being blasphemous, it was absolutely essential that Jesus was shown as being human so that we could share His human experience.

It is not difficult to see why the figure of Jesus should provide such an attractive topic for a playwright. Few, if any figures in history have been so copiously discussed in literature. Unlike the founders of any of the world's other faiths, Jesus emerges from the Gospels that tell of His life and teaching as a highly complex personality. For some He is a great story-teller, for others great teacher or worker of miracles. Some see Him as a fearless debater, others as a mystic. He was the friend of the dispossessed, the vulnerable and the outcast and yet, clearly had extensive support in intellectual and noble circles. His life was, in every sense, dramatic and yet the details we have of it are sufficiently sketchy and incomplete to tempt a writer to fill in the blanks. He was a revolutionary who challenged the status quo as every playwright seeks to do; His words have become part of our everyday speech in the way that only great dramatists and orators have shaped our language; He was able to command the attention of huge audiences to such an extent that they forgot that they were hungry and yet, in moments of one-to-one dialogue He could be the most engaging and affecting friend.

No actor could ever hope to impersonate Jesus in His entirety but aspects of His being are images that can be preserved and cultivated through drama. It is through images that human beings strive to make sense of their lives: these may be visual or verbal, tactile or auditory but, ultimately they are the means whereby we are enabled to use our 'imaginations' to take us beyond the mundane and humdrum towards something approaching the divine. The theatre brings together many diverse art forms and in this synthesis can provide an enrichment of life, belief and faith that has few equals.

CHAPTER TWO

The Jesus Of The Mysteries

For most people the idea of seeing a 'live' actor portraying or 'playing the part' of Jesus is probably associated with one of the spectacular 'Passion Plays' such as the production which takes place every ten years in Oberammergau. It is important to recognise that such dramas have their origins in very ancient traditions, especially in plays that were popular throughout Europe in the Middle Ages, and that those ancient plays showed Jesus in many situations other than his last few days on earth.

During the Middle Ages, especially at the Festival of Corpus Christi in Catholic countries, many cities and towns organised 'cycles' of plays that told the complete story of humankind's redemption from the time of the creation of the world to the last judgement. Because these plays were presented in many towns by the wealthy trade and crafts guilds they became known as 'Mystery Plays' from the old French word denoting 'the know-how'. However, the term 'Mystery' also implies that these short plays revealed the 'holy Mysteries' of the Christian faith. Some of the cycles contained upwards of thirty short plays and precisely how audiences managed to witness the entire sequence remains a matter of debate. We do know, however, that the plays were often presented on 'pageant wagons' that were taken through the streets rather like a carnival procession and that this means that they came very close to their audiences.

We can speculate that the plays were intended to show the complete story of God's plan revealed in both the Old and New Testaments to a largely illiterate audience. They familiarised their spectators with all the major characters of the

Bible and often reinforced important theological teachings. For example, the story of Abraham called upon to sacrifice his son Isaac prepared the onlookers for the later sacrifice of God's son on the cross.

Quite why these wonderful plays ceased to be part of the communal life of our towns and cities is not known. Because some similar plays have been regularly performed in mainly Catholic countries, scholars have attributed their disappearance in Britain and parts of Northern Europe to their being suppressed by the forces of the Protestant Reformation. They have argued that the plays were seen as being too 'Catholic' and too much associated with the perceived evils of the theatre. However, what we are now coming to realise is that our society was deprived for many years of one of the most vivid pictures of Jesus that the human imagination could conceive. Fortunately, however, some of the scripts of these plays did survive and we have complete or virtually complete cycles of plays from York, Chester, Wakefield and a Midlands town simply called 'N' Town that is usually assumed to have been Lincoln. There are also surviving parts of the Coventry cycle (containing the famous *Coventry Carol*) and fragments from Newcastle and Cornwall together with an impressive play of Abraham and Isaac which survived in a great house in Suffolk. All of the plays are anonymous but it is reasonable to assume that they may have been written by educated churchmen with a very thorough knowledge of scripture. It is almost certain that they were changed and adapted over the years and that they 'borrowed' heavily from each other. They were written almost entirely in verse and this was of variable quality. Some of the Wakefield plays are written with such a distinctive touch that their anonymous author had been called the *Wakefield Master* whereas one of the writers of the York plays had such a sense of realistic detail that he is known as the 'York realist'.

The Cornish Plays

One part of Britain that developed its own distinctive form of Christian drama was the ancient kingdom of Cornwall and records show that a type of Mystery play known as the

Ordinalia had its origins in the late fifteenth century. Written in the Cornish language, probably by the secular canons of Glasney College in Penryn, the *Ordinalia* was in three parts and required attendance on three consecutive occasions. Together these three sections, which may be translated as 'The Creation', 'The Passion' and 'The Resurrection', tell the complete story of our redemption and archaeologists have identified over eighty 'Plen an Gwary' (playing places) in which these plays might have been performed in Cornwall. The most completely preserved of such, usually circular, spaces is in St. Just-in-Penwith.

It may have been the decline of the Cornish language and the gradual influence of new religious ideas that led to the disappearance of these plays some time in the seventeenth century but as long ago as 1916 the scholar, T.Taylor was writing in his book *The Celtic Christianity of Cornwall* of the power of these plays in performance. Drawing on his experience of the revival of some plays in Brittany that appear to have had similar origins to the Cornish plays he, quite remarkably, identified one of the abiding problems of recent productions of 'religious drama'. He suggested that the Cornish dramas were performed with: "reverent adoring faith.....robust, inspiring patriotism, the utter absence of anything like vanity or pretence". (p.48)

He then goes on to remark that the plays preserved: "the intense reality of the Gospel story which, too often, in the case of ordinary Englishmen, has, under the soothing influence of an inimitable authorised version of Holy Scriptures, become an idyllic, poetical and idealistic presentment of Scriptural truth". (ibid.)

The tendency to idealise the portrayal of Jesus in drama has continued to provide a contentious issue for directors, actors and audiences. It was, however, nearly another ninety years after Taylor was writing, before the Cornish plays were seen again in their original settings. There had been a successful University production in New York before the First World War but plans to revive them in Cornwall were abandoned in 1915. However, in 1969, a production of the *Cornish Passion Play* took place in the Piran Round and then, at the Millenium, a project to produce all three parts of the

Ordinalia at St. Just was initiated, and a text was commissioned from the Cornish playwright, Pauline Sheppard that rendered the play comprehensible to modern audiences. The project culminated in 2004 when the complete cycle of plays was presented to audiences of many thousands and, subsequently another translation by the Cornish poet Alan Kent (2005) has brought these unique plays to a wider, reading public. The involvement of large sections of particular communities in the presentation of the Christian faith through drama has become, once again, a significant factor in empowering local Church and non-Church organisations and the bringing together of disparate talents in a single endeavour.

Reviving the Mysteries

Whereas the Cornish plays had to wait until the late twentieth and early twenty- first centuries for a revival it was towards the very end of the nineteenth century that a number of published versions of Mystery plays from other parts of Britain began to appear. It was not, however, until the early years of the twentieth century that a desire to produce the plays once more began to take hold with some drama enthusiasts. But there were three major obstacles to such ideas and ambitions. Firstly there was simply a matter of censorship. Until the office of the Lord Chamberlain was abolished in 1968, the representation of the deity in public performances was regarded as illegal. Any revival of the Mystery Plays with a living, breathing actor playing Jesus, however reverently, would have had to be in a private performance and, quite literally, the Jesus of the Mysteries might only be 'preaching to the converted'.

Private performances, not requiring a licence, had to take place largely in small halls or other 'found spaces' as they would now be called, and never in public theatres nor, indeed, great cathedrals.

But Christian prejudice towards the theatre extended even further and provided yet another stumbling block for those who wanted to see Jesus on stage. Even when, for example, the Dean of Canterbury Cathedral commissioned a new Nativity play in 1928 it was regarded by some clergy as the work of the devil and the actor who played the 'Anima Christi', a representation of Jesus before his incarnation, felt obliged to remain anonymous. Many years later, in the 1950s the Lord's Day Observance Society attempted to prosecute the producers of a Mystery Play for blasphemy.

In spite of such discouragements there were directors and actors who were determined that the powerful and profoundly attractive figure of Jesus as revealed in the Mystery Plays would be seen on stage again. Furthermore, some Cathedral cities came to the realisation that they were custodians of some of the most valuable of cultural and literary treasures and felt constrained to demonstrate that the Son of God, for whose worship the great cathedrals were built, could also be the Son of Man in a drama for all people. Even though York, Chester, Coventry and others embraced this idea and staged productions it was not until Canterbury created its own cycle by judicious selection of texts from other sources in 1986 that performances of the plays took place *inside* a cathedral rather than in the grounds or the ruins.

Before any productions could take place, however, there was one further problem: the scripts of the plays themselves. All that had survived were written in a form of language that would be virtually unintelligible to a modern audience and although experts recognised in the texts many sections of effective dialogue, lively poetry and memorable biblical language, it was necessary to embark on a process of adaptation and translation in order to create workable editions for actors and audiences. Remarkable scripts were, in fact, created by such experts as the Rev. J. Purvis for York (1951), Keith Miles for Coventry (1981), Maurice Hussey for Chester (1957), A.C. Cawley (1958) for Wakefield and more recently Douglas Sugano for 'N' town (1997). These were supplemented by a number of compilations of 'key' plays drawn from a single or several cycles welded together to create a single drama dealing with the life of Jesus. One of the most successful of these was *The Redemption* (1964) created by the actor and television news reader, Gordon Honeycombe, which tells of the events of the Saviour's Passion.

Perhaps the most significant moment in the rediscovery of medieval drama was the translation by the poet Tony Harrison (1977) of plays presented under the collective title of *The Mysteries* at the National Theatre in London. This drama in three parts : *The Creation*, *The Passion* and *Doomsday* required attendance on three separate occasions and from that moment, the words, actions and life of Jesus became a major talking point in the contemporary theatre. Through a televised version of the production and, subsequently during several revivals, *The Mysteries* brought the character of Jesus to the attention of many non-churchgoers and strengthened the faith of many for whom the Bible narrative was familiar.

So who *is* the Jesus of the Mystery Plays and how can He speak to modern audiences? In order to answer these questions let us provide a concrete example. Here are some words from the director of a fairly recent production of the *Mysteries* staged in various parts of Canterbury Cathedral. The play he refers to is the incident of the 'Raising of Lazarus' one of the plays seen in the crypt:

The dramatist Strindberg said he was writing for "Modern Man in a Hurry" and I suppose it was that 'modern' person we had in mind when we adapted the play of the Raising of Lazarus for presentation in Canterbury Cathedral and elsewhere. The original play contains a lengthy discourse on resurrection spoken by Lazarus himself after he has risen from the dead. We thought that audiences, saturated with reality would find that a particularly incredible response to so poignant a human drama so the play was much shortened and the focus shifted to Jesus himself and his assurances to Mary and Martha. Yet, strangely, no play in performance brought us closer to the Timeless and the Eternal and in the sepulchral gloom of the crypt the words of Jesus in sublime paraphrase of the scriptures seemed like a sudden illumination:

> I tell you all, both man and wife,
> I am the resurrection and the life,
> And whoso truly believes in me,
> That I was ever and aye shall be,

One thing I shall him give,
Though he be dead, yet shall he live.

In a recent manual on playwriting Shelly Frome urges
would-be playwrights to seek out primitive and timeless
spaces to give them inspiration and I think it was one of
those glimpses of Eternity which led us to select the crypt for
this particular play. In this 'found space' the play was
presented 'in the round', the audience seated on simple
benches among the great arches and the actors in the midst.
The stillness and the quiet weeping of Mary added to the
sense that we had all gathered to meditate on mortality. The
shrouded figure of Lazarus lay white in the dim light and
when Jesus entered he seemed to have come from an
echoing distance.

Human beings often rage against Jesus in the face of
suffering and Martha is no exception:

> Help me Lord in most need!
> Lazarus, my brother, now is dead,
> That was to thee both loved and dear;
> He had not died had thou been here.

Jesus' reply is strong, personal and gentle:

> Martha, Martha, from grief refrain,
> Thy brother shall live and rise again.

It is only then that Jesus addresses the entire audience with
the words of such startling authority that actors found
almost too charged to speak:

> I tell you all, both man and wife,
> I am the resurrection and the life!

But the playwright has more for us: he goes deep to the root
of our lack of faith and hope. Both Martha and Mary reveal
an uncertainty that Jesus has to challenge before He can act.
Jesus will not be satisfied until His friends acknowledge that
there is *nothing* he cannot do. He, the embodiment of
Eternal Life, is the constant hope to which we must all
respond:

> Hither we are come to you,
> To bring you comfort in your care.
> But look that faint heart nor no sloth
> Takes you from the steadfast truth.

Nevertheless, Jesus shares the sufferings of His friends: he is deeply moved by the death of Lazarus and even more by the distress of Mary and Martha. He blends authority with comfort. In one sense the details of the biblical narrative become irrelevant and, indeed, although the moment of resurrection was such that it was witnessed by the audience with a degree of concentration I have rarely seen in the theatre, it was as if Lazarus himself was no longer relevant. At its ultimate level the play is not about the raising of an obscure man of whom we know virtually nothing, it is about the idea of hope in a living God. Of course, as part of a cycle of plays, it prefigures the resurrection of Jesus but it also wrestles with ideas central to the human predicament: certainty, doubt, faith, love, compassion, grief, joy: all set against the magnitude of the Transcendent who, in this supreme Mystery, become Immanent.

In the original text Martha speaks a quaint epilogue. After the remarkable events we have witnessed it seems small-scale yet it is a still small voice in which she shares her faith with the audience and seeks to pass on the loving and healing spirit of her Master.

> He is a Lord of Grace.
> Meditate on this case,
> And pray him, full of might,
> He keep you in this place,
> And have you in his sight.[1]

So Jesus emerges from this play as a complex, commanding and attractive character. We can see, for example, that the words of Jesus are based directly on words from the Bible yet have a distinct quality of their own. We see, also, that the action of such plays is by no means confined to the events of Christ's Passion. The director writing here comes from a generation and church-going background that tends to be very familiar with the Authorised Version of the Bible and is clearly at home with such concepts as Eternal Life, Resurrection and Salvation. But what if the audience shared

1   Kenneth Pickering (1990) in *Peter Smith of Churchman*

none of these factors or were only familiar with Scripture in very modern translation? Further questions are posed by the use of a 'sacred space' for the re-enactment of great truths and myths which is common to religious observance and theatre. At what point do the spectators become worshippers; or are they both?

As we attempt to answer these and other important questions if will be helpful if we consider some of the other Mystery Plays in which Jesus appears as an important character.

Jesus speaks

The first play in which Jesus actually speaks is based on that tantalising sole glimpse we have of His boyhood recorded in *St. Luke's Gospel*. At one level this is a very human story of every parent's nightmare: a child goes missing. The young, twelve-year-old Jesus is taken by his mother and father to Jerusalem for the Passover Festival and they travel with a crowd of friends and neighbours. It is only on the way home that Mary and Joseph realise that Jesus, whom they assumed to be with the crowd, is in fact not present and, in desperation, they return to the city to look for him. They eventually find Jesus in the Temple, sitting with a group of religious teachers, listening, asking questions and astonishing everyone by his intelligence and understanding. When His mother asks Jesus why He has caused His parents so much concern he replies enigmatically: "How is it that ye sought me? Wist ye not that I must be about my Father's business?" (AV) or, as the *Good News* Bible puts it: "Why did you have to look for me? Didn't you know that I had to be in my Father's house?"

Quite understandably, his parents simply don't understand His reply!

That play of what is usually known as 'Christ and the Doctors' appears in a number of the cycles and is probably best explored in the lively translation that the playwright and novelist Keith Miles made for Coventry. The problem of the story for the original playwrights was that there is so little detail in the biblical narrative. What, for example, did Jesus discuss with the teachers; what were His answers and why did

He give such a cool response to His parents? In order to bring this particular story to life on stage the answers to such questions must be provided by the playwright's imagination. So that for instance the discussion between Jesus and the teachers or the moment when His parents realise He is missing can seem *real*. Thus, both dialogue and events may have to be invented to flesh out the bare bones of the Bible story.

In the Coventry play we see Jesus with His parents preparing to leave for Jerusalem and, as in many plays, it is what is said about Jesus that is particularly significant. Joseph and Mary are heard discussing their son's special qualities and His readiness to take part in the holiest of ceremonies. It comes as no surprise to the audience that the young Jesus appears both charmingly obedient and almost precociously confident:

> Now come on, mother, and fear you nought.
> Begin your journey, as you ought,
> The Father in Heaven that all has wrought,
> May He keep you from distress.

This small speech provokes an almost incredulous Joseph to remark how much more grown up and sophisticated children now seem compared with when he was a boy. It was ever thus! Whereas the Bible story simply tells us that the family *made* the journey, the Medieval playwright *shows* us the journey, with Joseph finding his legs aching and a fascinated Jesus wanting to explore the temple. The solemn ceremonies ended, Mary and Joseph set off on their homeward journey discussing their experience and only after a while do they realise that Jesus is not with them and decide to retrace their steps. At that point the scene shifts back to the temple and to a group of learned doctors of the law. Which of us who have read or heard this one story of Jesus as a boy has not wondered what it was that He said that so impressed His listeners? But for believers it is even more important to ask what members of an audience who do *not* know the story take away from a performance of the play. An actor, playwright or director must always work on the assumption that an audience is encountering a story for the first time and the Medieval writer gives memorable and vivid images of the young Jesus confidently approaching and greeting a group of doctors of the law:

> Lords, much love be with you now
> And peace among this company!

The three learned men make the excuse that they are far too busy for chat and, besides, Jesus is far too young to understand the Law of Moses. Jesus, however, stuns them with His reply, telling them first that He has nothing to learn from them and then, when they object, that He understands the Law perfectly because He comes from the very place where it originated. So the playwright gives us a picture of a twelve-year-old, already aware of His own destiny and divinity and totally familiar with the nuances of the religious beliefs and practices of His day. The portrait of a remarkable boy is further enhanced as the doctors insist that Jesus sits with them in discourse. In answer to their first enquiry, which is about the source of His learning and understanding, Jesus clams that it is the Holy Ghost and then expounds on the idea that He existed before the world began and would continue to do so! Reacting to the baffled response Jesus tells the doctors that He can show them many Mysteries but they obviously feel that they will be on safer ground if they restrict their discussion to the Law and Commandments.

The incident we have just outlined provides an example of the intent and technique of these glorious plays from the Middle Ages. Their purpose was clearly to *teach* and to explain the meaning of the scriptures. Accordingly there is some use of artistic licence and use of anachronism. The coming of the Holy Ghost, for example, is described in the Bible as having followed the death, resurrection and ascension of Jesus but here He is already empowered by the Holy Ghost. On the other hand, and far more important than the sequential detail, Jesus introduces the concept that in the Godhead, He, His Father and the Holy Ghost are *One*.

Jesus is supremely self-assured in dealing with the doctors. When they challenge Him to say which is the first commandment He replies by suggesting that, since they have the books open in front of them, they tell Him! In fact, they do name and elaborate on the first two commandments until they recover their composure and ask Jesus to continue. Inevitably, Jesus is not only able to recite the remaining eight commandments but to provide a commentary on them that would do credit to any modern, scholarly preacher. In a sense, Jesus has begun His ministry.

Just before the anxious Mary and Joseph arrive to be reunited with their son one of the doctors comments that it were best if their exchange with Jesus were kept quiet for fear that the public will take more heed of Jesus than of them and, in this way, the play hints at conflicts to come.

The conclusion of the play reverts to very human touches that enable it to communicate directly to the lives and experience of the audience. An emotional Mary is overjoyed to see her son and urges Joseph to extract Him from the circle of doctors. But the self-effacing and status-conscious Joseph is reluctant because he feels so out of place in such company. When Mary exclaims the equivalent of "Oh, all right, I'll do it!" we know that it will be to her that Jesus will make His final, enigmatic statement before taking leave of the doctors:

> Mother, why did you seek me so?
> It has often been said unto you
> My Father's wish I must fulfil
> In every point, for good or ill.

Joseph makes a last aside to the audience about the necessity of keeping one's wife happy as the family departs leaving the doctors discussing and pondering the qualities of the young Jesus.

So we see that, not only has the dramatist compressed the events of three days into a fifteen minute play and pointed the theological lessons of the Trinity and the Law but has also transformed the sketchy biblical narrative into a fascinating and compelling portrait of Jesus.

We have spent some time considering this short play because it provides an excellent example of a playwright with an evangelical intention. We may not know who wrote the original play but the writer was clearly familiar with and anxious to promote the doctrines of the Church. However, by giving Jesus a distinctive personality and sense of divinity these early dramatists brought the Bible stories to life and made the divine accessible and human.

Jesus is tested

After a sequence of plays that has introduced such diverse and memorable characters as Adam and Eve, Satan, Cain and Abel, Moses, Balaam and his ass and the Prophets, the central character of the story of Redemption - the adult Jesus, makes His first appearance in the play of John the Baptist. Perhaps the most dramatic features of Jesus and, hence of the actor playing Him, are his stillness and silent entrances and we experience them in this play. Even though the coming of Jesus has been prepared for in the previous play He does not arrive spectacularly. Indeed, He arrives quietly and unobtrusively and many Christians would say that he continues to do so. Jesus simply joins the queue in the crowd awaiting baptism from John after the Baptist has preached a fiery sermon. It is only when Jesus and John come face to face that the drama takes on the intensity of a great encounter.

For audiences seeing one of the modern adaptations of the Mystery Plays this is also their first glimpse of the actor who will play the part of Jesus through His subsequent life, death and resurrection and that actor may well become an image of the living Jesus that will stay with them. There is some evidence that in the Middle Ages, the part of Jesus was played by a succession of actors because each play about His life was staged by a different Trade or Church Guild. This, of course, provided a very different experience for audiences and Jesus, perhaps would have been seen more as a 'figure' and less as a 'character' just as He is sometimes represented in Medieval paintings or icons. The whole debate about 'playing Jesus', was brought into relief in more recent times in 1992, when the Canterbury production of *The Mysteries* used three different actors to play the part in order to enable the audience to move between various locations. Many of the audience testified to the richness of the experience of seeing several 'faces' of Jesus.

The play of John the Baptist occurs in very similar forms in a number of cycles and all recent adaptations have felt the need for substantial cutting and reordering of the material because it is so wordy and loaded with exposition of theological doctrine. As with the 'Lazarus' play, our current less literary and more visual world tends to focus our drama on action and tension and it is these moments that emerge powerfully in performance.

When John finds Jesus standing before him as a figure of calm authority he recognises Him as someone from heaven who ought to be baptising and not receiving baptism. Jesus, however, gently but firmly insists on being baptised and explains the significance of that sacrament to all His listeners. The moment of Jesus' immersion is accompanied by celestial singing as, strangely to modern ears interested in historical accuracy, Jesus is baptised in the name of the Father, the Son and the Holy Ghost. Jesus then gives words of encouragement and command to 'go forth once more to preach' and leaves John watching His departure. The wonderful words with which John bids his Lord farewell are a fine example of the way in which an important character is built up by what is said *about* them. These lines in Keith Miles' translation for Coventry constitute a rewarding moment for any actor in performance.

> Farewell, sweet saviour of those forlorn.
> Farewell, the steersman of those by
> storms and sorrows beset.
> Farwell, redeemer of mankind's woe!
> Great glory be with you wherever you go!
> Farewell, my master, Lord and king,
> Farewell my friend,
> I follow you in everything,
> Unto the end!

Actors, critics, playwrights and directors have always understood that conflict is an essential ingredient of drama. In the drama of Jesus that conflict is provided by two Mystery Plays that are linked in theme and often performed sequentially. They show Jesus put to the test as He embarks on His ministry and, perhaps unexpectedly, introduce elements of farce and humour into the action.

The first of these two plays shows the Temptation of Jesus. The Bible story tells how, following His baptism, Jesus went into the wilderness and was tempted by the Devil. Firstly He is tempted to assuage His hunger by turning stones into bread; secondly to perform a populist 'miracle' by jumping from the pinnacle of the temple and, thirdly to worship the Devil in return for lordship over all the land visible from the summit of the highest mountain. Jesus rebuffs all three temptations.

In the Mystery play the Devil comes leaping out of hot, tormenting hell and shares with the audience his intention of ensnaring Jesus,(for whom he has created the nickname 'dosey beard') with his trickery. Satan complains that the teaching and deeds of Jesus have already undermined his evil kingdom and approaches Him slyly and unctuously. The sparks begin to fly in the heated exchanges between Jesus and Satan: each temptation is met with an increasingly stern riposte. When, finally, Satan takes Jesus to a high point to show Him all the kingdoms of this world, the ferocity of Christ's response sends him reeling. This is a fine example of a situation in which the meaning of the Medieval text was so obvious in performance that, when it was used at Canterbury in recent productions it was found unnecessary to 'translate' it into modern English:

> Go forth Satan ! Go forth, Go!
> It is written and shall be so,
> God, thy Lord, thou shalt honour mo
> And serve Him though it thee noye.

The devil's capering, cowering and ingratiation are comical and in direct contrast to the stern, Scripture-based authority of Jesus. Satan realises he is beaten and makes a hasty retreat. Mockery is one way in which we come to terms with evil.

Jesus reveals the same ability to recognise and respond to a potential trap in the play of the 'Woman taken in Adultery' which forms a thematic pair with the 'Temptation'. Although versions of this play appear in several of the cycles it is the play from 'N' Town that best brings out the drama of the situation and provides some of the most memorable moments and lines in English drama. Once again the audience sees the plot being hatched before seeing Jesus. A group of religious leaders, usually described as Pharisees, are complaining, like Satan, that this upstart Jesus the mere son of a shepherd's daughter (according to them) is negating their authority and teaching. They reveal that they know that a young man and a married woman are having an illicit affair and that they would be able to catch them in the very act. If they can then take them to Jesus for judgement, He will, they imagine, have no option but to uphold the law of Moses that insists on the woman's being stoned to death. This will severely test Jesus and His doctrines of mercy and compassion.

There now follows a moment of pure farce: the plotters burst in on the lovers and the young man emerges attempting to hold up his trousers whilst threatening his tormentors with a knife. The intruders scatter while the wretched man runs off and then, hurling insults at her, they drag out the pleading woman and throw her at the feet of Jesus who has silently entered. The Pharisees each attempt to elicit a response from Jesus but He remains utterly silent, writing with His finger in the sand. As His tempters employ every possible tactic and verbal ploy to ensnare Jesus one of them describes Him as being in a 'cold study' as He squats motionless and impassive. The Pharisees grow increasingly frustrated but Jesus dramatically breaks the silence, looking up and inviting the person without sin to throw the first stone. As He resumes writing in the sand the accusers slink away one by one, leaving Jesus and the woman together at the same eye level. At this point we see another aspect of the character of Jesus. With great tenderness He asks where the accusers have gone and when she replies that they have left He lifts her up and sends her on her way with the injunction to 'sin no more'. This striking and moving image shows the Saviour lifting sinful humankind out of misery into new life and through the knockabout and verbal trickery encapsulates the ideas of hope and compassion that characterise the Jesus whose wisdom and intelligence can outwit any tempter.

'The Raising of Lazarus' appears in all the cycles and usually grows out of other plays that focus on Jesus as a teacher, preacher and healer. Jesus is shown restoring sight to the blind and mending the broken spirit of Mary Magdalene as she pours costly ointment over His feet and wipes them with her long hair. We hear Jesus reprimanding Judas for his cynical attitudes towards Mary's act of adoration and penitence and, above all, we hear Him preaching.

The Medieval plays used what may seem rather random verse paraphrases of some of the recorded words of Jesus as examples of His preaching. They give Him few of His dramatic parables and little of His more powerful rhetoric or revolutionary social teaching. In comparison with His demolition of His detractors the preaching of Jesus may seem to a modern audience somewhat one dimensional. In fact, we detect more of the doctrine of the Catholic Church in Christ's preaching than we recognise some of His graphic illustrations of God's love.

However, there is one interesting exception in the sustained passage of preaching in the Chester cycle when brilliantly adapted by the former ITN newsreader Gordon Honeycombe as part of his compilation *The Redemption*. Jesus tells His audience that He is the Son of God, the Light of the World and the Good Shepherd. He urges His listeners to follow His teaching and to be recognised as belonging to His 'family'. He explains that He and the Father are 'one' and that He was promised for the world's salvation from before the beginning of time. Jesus declares that He is to embark on a life of healing and teaching in fulfilment of Scriptural prophecy. Throughout this particular play the image of Light is dominant. Not only does Jesus restore sight to the blind but He constantly refers to those who prefer to walk in darkness than follow the 'Light of the World'.

The earthly Jesus

We have seen that, in the play of the 'Woman taken in Adultery' Jesus was dismissed as the son of a shepherd's daughter. This is one of many examples of the Medieval playwrights setting the plays in *their* world rather than striving for strict scriptural accuracy. Their intention is clear: to make Jesus relevant to the audiences of the day, something which, perhaps, the modern Church singularly fails to do.

The Bible makes no suggestion that Mary was a shepherd's daughter but every member of the audience in the Middle Ages would know that, in a society of which the very economic foundation was wool, there were few more lowly jobs than that of a shepherd. Rich wool merchants may have financed the building of great churches but little of that wealth trickled down to ordinary people. The image of Jesus as the Good Shepherd would not be lost on the audiences of the oppressed. For the same reasons the Medieval Nativity plays contained comic shepherds with names such as Mak, Coll and Gib, bewailing their lot, cursing the inclement weather, sharing their picnics and much vulgar banter and even stealing the odd sheep. The names of the shepherds, as were those of the accusers and detractors of Jesus, were not biblical but contemporary. All such homely details served a single purpose, and they still do, to remind audiences that the Son of God who liked to call himself the 'Light of the World' or 'Good Shepherd' walked this earth as a man and shared in the world's humour and sufferings. But, just as there are still those who would rather cling to outmoded attitudes and rules rather than embrace new concepts and ideas, so in drama those forces who prefer to remain in darkness reach their climax in Christ's Passion.

The continuing power of the Mystery Plays to engage, move and deepen the faith of audiences is illustrated by one of the most recent productions staged in the ruins of Monk Bretton Priory in 2009. Inspired by the Bishop of Wakefield (one of the cities with its own Mystery Cycle) the play was initially conceived as a joint community and English Heritage project to regenerate the ruined buildings. The reaction of the Bishop to seeing the production created by the writer and director John Kelly was that it was "more powerful as a piece of apologetics than anything I had seen for the past five or ten years". Significantly he added, "Even though it's being put on by a secular organisation, it has real impact". The Bishop goes on to draw attention to both the humour and pathos of the production and makes special mention of the Passion. Like many 'Mystery' productions a famous voice, in this case that of Patrick Stewart of *Star Trek*, represented God and it is possible to sense that it was precisely because the production was *not* entirely in the hands of believers and that it impinged on the world of popular media entertainment that it emanated an energy and directness that comes from a community sharing its humanity rather than its particular faith.

The process whereby a community becomes involved in the production of a Mystery Play Cycle and its impact on the participants are fascinatingly explored in Peter Gill's (2001) play *The York Realist*. The play takes its title from the name that has sometimes been assigned to the anonymous author of the York Mystery Plays which show the events surrounding the crucifixion of Jesus with particular and horrifying realism. Set in 1960, *The York Realist* shows the effect on a farm worker, George, whose non-conformist, chapel-going family have persuaded to take part in the York Mystery Plays and who has been cast as one of the torturers who help to crucify Jesus. The play opens with a visit to the farm house by John, the Assistant Director from the London theatre who has noticed that George has ceased attending rehearsals. John assures George that he has considerable acting talent (a situation that has been fairly frequently repeated with the huge and unusual amateur casts assembled to help stage such productions) but the real issue turns out to be the growing love between the two men that neither really knows how to handle. We see the progress of the production with George reinstated in his role and the reaction of his scripturally-saturated family to the performances which they find deeply moving and satisfying, but we also see the love story unfolding and the lack of realism in John's expectations of George. Although George briefly goes to London and is tempted by the theatre and arts scene, he realises that his involvement in the Mystery Plays has, in fact, been a brief foray into a world that, whilst extending his horizons, is unattainable. The play is a poignant reminder of the sometimes delicate interaction between the professional theatre and the use of drama as a means of expressing Christian belief.

CHAPTER THREE

The Jesus Of The Passions

The drama of the Passion of Christ is not confined to the theatre or media. Painters, sculptors, novelists and composers have all been drawn to the subject and it has undoubtedly provided the inspiration for some of the world's greatest works of art.

The events that took place during what the Church often calls Holy Week have particular significance for Christians. Beginning with Jesus riding a donkey into Jerusalem to the applause of a crowd on Palm Sunday and culminating in His dead body being laid in a new tomb. This week includes the inauguration of the most solemn and debated ceremony in the entire Christian world on Maundy Thursday and the sacrificial death of Jesus by crucifixion on Good Friday. The so-called 'Last Supper' and its development into the Communion or the Mass and the concept of Jesus dying on the cross for the sins of the world have become two of the central beliefs of many millions of Christians and the various branches of the Church have always seen it as essential to promote these tenets of faith. Furthermore, a belief in the miraculous Resurrection of Jesus after His death has become not only the pivotal belief of most forms of Christianity but also the most widely celebrated aspect of Jesus through the arts of performance, theatre and carnival.

In predominantly Roman Catholic countries the Passion and the Festivals of Easter and Corpus Christi (50 days later) are still widely and enthusiastically celebrated in dramatic form through carnival-like processions and ritual re-enactments. Many such celebrations, even in the smallest communities, involve the use of pageant wagons or floats on which

statues of Jesus, Mary and the saints are mounted and vener-
ated. Some involve sequences of scenes depicting such
events as the Last Supper, Jesus in Gethsemane or His
scourging. However, a large proportion of these evocations
of the events of Holy Week stop short of having an actor representing Christ and rely on the symbolic presence of Jesus
in the 'host', the sacred bread of the Mass or on devotions to
the three dimensional images of Christ on the cross.

Throughout the Christian world, be it Catholic,
Orthodox or Protestant there are many dramatic re-enactments of Jesus carrying His own cross on a journey towards
death. This rudimentary form of street theatre is widely used
as a means of witness particularly when ordinary members of
the public 'take up the cross' and carry it. Probably the most
widely known example of this is undertaken by numerous
faith groups through the streets of old Jerusalem following
the so-called 'Via Dolorosa' - the Way of Sorrows.

On the Greek island of Corfu a truly remarkable drama
takes place during Holy Week culminating in a crescendo of
light and sound as the risen Christ is welcomed just after the
stroke of midnight on Easter Day. On Good Friday the
narrow streets of Corfu town are the setting for many solemn
processions. Every church in the town parades its *epitafios*,
the holy table bearing the image of Jesus and shaped like a
symbolic bier carried on the shoulders of mourners and
beautifully decorated with flowers. Each of these processions, made up of all manner of uniformed organisations
and representatives of all ages, winds its way slowly through
the streets, led by a band and often the sound of muffled
drums. Moving with a strange slow march in which both
arms are swung together in the same direction, the people of
the procession will walk throughout the entire afternoon
and on into the evening until the procession of the *epitafios*
of the Cathedral sets out on its journey around the town led
by the gorgeously attired Metropolitan and his priests and
accompanied by many mourners carrying candles. As with
so many Passion remembrances this is truly a community
event and leads to yet more symbolic happenings in the following two days. For many, the final climax is the family
gathering in the olive groves or homes for feasting on the

paschal lamb. Although Jesus is not represented by an actor
His presence is unavoidable throughout the images and
symbols that seem to unite a community in their faith.

Passion Plays and their musical equivalents

Passion Plays can be found in many forms and invariably
they appear to have had ancient origins. The most extensive
of the Mystery Play cycles all contained substantial groups of
plays relating to the Passion, usually constituting the largest
single section of the entire cycle. However, some surviving
Passion Plays from the Middle Ages appear to have
developed independently of larger cycles and to have been
popular in communities as folk plays throughout Europe. In
many parts of Spain, France and Eastern Europe such plays
continue to be performed in an unbroken tradition as an
essential ingredient of Catholic devotion.

But for many Protestant Christians such re-enactments of
the Passion with their statues, icons, images or performers
were seen, and sometimes still are, as idolatrous. Certainly,
by the beginning of the eighteenth century, the performance of Passion Plays was largely unknown in Protestant
Northern Europe or North America. Yet how were such
Christians to remind themselves of the biblical events and
times of the year that were at the very heart of their belief in
Jesus, the Saviour of the World? The answer lay in music and
in the development of a new form of music in particular: the
oratorio. Driven by the constant demand of the Lutheran
Church for the composition of new choral music for each
Sunday of the year, German composers began to create
pieces which, as the term 'oratorio' implies, told the great
stories of the Bible. Pre-eminent among these composers
was J.S. Bach whose great 'Passions' the *St. Matthew* and *St.
John* represent two of the mountain peaks of Christian art.
These works were, in almost every sense, dramas. They
introduced memorable characters: Peter, Pilate, a servant
girl who recognised Peter in the crowd, the High Priest and,
above all, Jesus Himself. With an Evangelist as narrator and
soloists singing the dialogue drawn directly from the
Gospels, the 'action' of the pieces was commented upon by a
chorus reminiscent of Greek tragedy. Evocative instrumen-

tal music not only accompanied the singers but also under-scored and suggested the events, such as the brutal hammering of nails into the hands and feet of Jesus. In fact, the entire story of Holy Week unfolded in the imaginations of the listeners through these remarkable musical Passions, and other composers saw the potential of the form.

Bach's Passions fell into neglect and were lost for nearly two hundred years, and the rediscovery of the *St. Matthew* in the nineteenth century by the composer Mendelssohn led not only to subsequent performances but also to the compo-sition of other Bible based oratorios, of which Mendels-sohn's own *Elijah* and *St. Paul* were dramatic and popular examples. In recent years, Bach's Passions have been recog-nised as so inherently 'theatrical' that a number of successful attempts have been made to stage them both in theatres and on television. In these works, Jesus is invariably represented by a performer with a powerful, commanding and lyrical bass voice whereas the Evangelist is a lighter-voiced, but no less expressive, tenor.

In the Victorian age and on into the twentieth century many church choirs had ambitions to perform musical Passions but found the works of Bach and his contemporar-ies too long and too difficult. Accordingly, a number of less demanding and smaller-scaled works were composed to cater mainly for the devotions of Protestant Christians during Holy Week and, indeed, some of these works continue to be performed at this time.

These more modest works were known as Cantatas, simply implying that they are sung and the two that made the greatest impact were *The Crucifixion* with music by John Stainer and words by J. Sparrow Simpson and *From Olivet to Calvary* composed by J.H. Maunder with words by Shapcot Wensley. Interestingly, these works are invariably known as 'Stainer's' or 'Maunder's' without any mention of the writers and compilers of the text. Both these cantatas contain beau-tiful hymns for singing by an otherwise passive and listening congregation and follow the example of Bach by containing dialogue, narration, crowd scenes, meditations on the sig-nificance of events and scenic music.

The Crucifixion begins its action in Gethsemane and we hear Jesus reprimanding His sleeping disciples and, later, in discourse with the High Priest or with the thieves on the cross. His progress to Calvary carrying His cross is marked by a haunting march motif and the darkness which follows His death is evoked by deep, dark rumblings on the organ pedals. Maunder, on the other hand, begins his narrative with Jesus entering Jerusalem from the Mount of Olives and weeping over the city, Probably unbeknown to countless devout listeners, Maunder was also a theatre composer and his flair for the dramatic becomes obvious in his handling of the incident when Jesus drove the money-changers out of the temple or when the crowd call for His death. Maunder did not hesitate either to employ music that reflected some of the popular music of his day.

Both works achieved a very high level of popularity for much of the twentieth century and fine sound recordings still exist. However, they undoubtedly promoted a somewhat sentimental view of Jesus:

> 'How sweet is the grace of His sacred face!'
>
> [*The Crucifixion*]

Or

> 'And Jesus paused and gazed with tearful eyes while the hushed multitude stood wondering near'
>
> [*From Olivet to Calvary*]

Even at the height of their popularity these two cantatas suffered from the lazy dismissiveness of so-called 'professional' church musicians, but what such critics failed to recognise was the extent to which the writers transformed their listeners into spectators in the theatre of the imagination, and hence into worshippers who identified and suffered with Jesus, the protagonist:

> Ye who sin and ye who sorrow,
> Ye who in temptation fall,
> See, O see your blest redeemer
> Standing in the judgement hall.
> See Him beaten and derided,
> See his flesh by scourges torn,

Turn to Him remembering ever
'Twas for you,' 'twas for you,
The pain was borne.

[From Olivet to Calvary]

Such musical substitutes for the physical theatre were joined by a number of similar pieces including *The Saviour* by W.S. Lloyd Webber, whose son Andrew would soon challenge the entire concept of the theatrical Jesus with his rock-opera *Jesus Christ Superstar*.

Once the legal objections to representing Christ onstage had been removed theatre practitioners were free to explore once again the most substantial and fascinating examples of Jesus as a dramatic figure capable of interpretation and presentation by an actor. These were to be found in the Mystery Plays and especially in some of their modern translations and adaptations. They present an altogether more robust and variable image of Jesus than do the Victorian cantatas and, at times, leave very little to the imagination.

Exploring the 'N' town cycle

The 'N' Town cycle grouped all the plays relating to the Passion of Christ in a separate book and in modern versions these provide some of the most stimulating and imaginative views of Jesus ever created. The plays were originally introduced by 'Banns' which spell out for the audience the scope of the material to follow and Douglas Sugano provides a translation that captures the spirit of great mysteries that are to unfold.

The Banns are called out to the audience by a series of Banner bearers, each of whom may represent a different group responsible for the presentation of plays. Between them they announce eight pageants of short plays that the audience is about to see. This may strike modern readers as strange but it is, in fact, no stranger than the practice of 'soap' producers who give us details of the 'story so far' and 'to come in this week's episodes'. Indeed, when we recall that these plays were to be performed to a largely illiterate audience with no access to 'programme notes' or the possibility of reading the story for themselves it is a perfectly understandable device that would greatly reinforce the learning and memory of the people watching. Such teaching aids were quite common in the Middle Ages: for example, the 'Sans Day Carol' and the catchy 'The seven joys of Mary' which date from this period, both take their singers and listeners through the major events in the life of Jesus and point out their significance for the salvation of humankind.

The first play listed in the Banns is *Conspiracy and Palm Sunday*, the second is predicted as showing, "Christ and His apostles all in sorrow, the maundy of God" and both the plotting of the rulers and Judas' initial betrayal. The third pageant describes the events in Gethsemane when. "Christ shall pray....that pain to cease" and will show the ultimate betrayal of Jesus with a kiss and the fleeing disciples. Pageant four we are told, will show Christ before Caiaphas, Herod and Pilate and Peter's denial of his master. The fifth pageant is to deal with the dreams of Pilate's wife and her plea to save the life of Jesus but we are also to see how the Jews prevent such mercy and refuse Pilate's offer to release Jesus and crucify Barabbas. In the sixth pageant, the Banns tell us that we shall witness Christ's crucifixion and hear His seven last words from the cross together with His injunction to John to care for His mother Mary. The material predicted for the seventh pageant is largely not sourced from the Gospels for it shows the scene of Jesus descending into and routing the forces of Hell. The 'Harrowing of Hell' will also include the coming of Joseph of Arimathea and Nicodemus to take the body of Jesus to the tomb and the consternation of Pilate and Caiaphas when they hear news of Christ's disappearance from that tomb; the soldiers are bribed to remain silent. The final play will deal with the risen Christ and His appearances to Mary Magdalene, Thomas and to other disciples and will culminate in His Ascension.

Having told the audience in some detail what they are to expect, one of the Banner bearers concludes:

> Now that we have told you all indeed
> The whole matter that we think to play,
> When that ye come here shall ye see
> The game well played in good array.
> Of Holy Writ this game shall been,
> And of no fables be no way.

> Now God them save from harm and grief
> For us that prayeth upon that day,
> And requite them well their meed.

What may seem to us to be a rather quaint mixture of fun and seriousness and an introduction that is not entirely accurate in its claim to be entirely scriptural must not obscure the fact that, even today, these are powerful and moving dramas. Fortunately for those of us who wish to present these remarkable pieces of theatre to modern audiences, we also have some details of the way in which they were originally staged and find them almost filmic in the manner in which the scenes cut one to another and are interwoven with continuous action taking place in various imaginary locations. For example, Douglas Sugano's version of the 'N' Town Passion suggests:

> *The Passion stage consists of a scaffolding complex of stages for Annas, Caiaphas, Herod, Pilate and their cohorts. Different stages have their own curtains and are all inter-connected by ramps or steps: Pilate's is higher than Herod's; Herod's higher than Caiaphas's; Caiaphas's higher than Annas's. A large playing area contains the Jewish Council House where the Sanhedrin meetings take place.*

We then have an indication of the way in which producers in the Middle Ages attempted to make the plays relevant to their audiences:

> *Annas is dressed as a fifteenth-century judge-scarlet gown, blue tabard furred with white. He and Caiaphas are attended by their Lawyers who apper with furred gowns and furred caps. Arfex[2] is attired as a Saracen.*

We shall see the multi-focus staging at work from the very outset of the Passion when, in an unexpected moment, Satan leaps out of a Hell mouth and, in very long speech directed at the audience with whom he mingles, explains how Jesus has thwarted all his intentions by the power of His righteousness and how he is now plotting to bring about His downfall. Satan asks for the audiences' loyalty and, rather like a comic figure in a Christmas pantomime, tells them that, although he is going off-stage for a while, he will always

---

2   an invented messenger/plotter figure

come if they call! The action then shifts to the Council House where the Sanhedrin (dressed, as we have seen, in contemporary costumes) are plotting to do Satan's work in destroying Jesus. The chief complaints against Jesus are that He 'showeth miracles' and that some people call Him 'Son of God'. A further charge is that Jesus has called Himself King of the Jews and, thus, they believe, He can be labelled a traitor. The accusations and plans to spy on Jesus reach an almost hysterical climax as the curtain on the Council House closes.

All this has prepared for the entry of Jesus Himself, metaphorically riding into a storm. The stage is transformed into a positive and jubilant place as the crowd welcomes Jesus mounted on His foal by throwing flowers, branches and garments to strew His way. The scene, in fact, is set for one of a number of great speeches that characterise Jesus in the Passions and make playing the role of Jesus so rewarding and challenging for actors. Such speeches stand out from the surrounding dialogue by their calm emotional simplicity and depth. They show Jesus acutely aware of His destiny and purpose and the cosmic significance of His life: in this case 'a cord betwixt God and man'. Jesus paints a picture of His mission as a constant struggle with Satan, (of whom the audience has recently been reminded) and with the 'Prince of this World' represented by the cunning of the lawyers and religious leaders of His day. In a striking image of His ability to open people's eyes to the reality of the Kingdom of Heaven Jesus concludes the first pageant by healing two blind beggars who have pushed their way through the crowds.

The second pageant begins as Jesus goes on His way and pauses to weep over Jerusalem. His lamentation is one of the finest and most moving speeches in the whole of English drama and, like His earlier speech to the crowd, is an extended paraphrase of Scripture. Not only is this a poignant speech it is also one of the supreme moments of theatre that increasingly draw us to the character of Jesus for now we see His emotional life revealed in His private musings. This is the forerunner of the technique of the 'soliloquy' developed so brilliantly by Marlowe and Shakespeare

The Jesus Of The Passions

as a means of enabling the audience to eavesdrop on some of a character's innermost thoughts:

> O Jerusalem, woeful is thy ordinance
> On the day of thy great persecution!
> Thou shalt be destroyed with
> woeful grievance,
> And thy royalty brought to
> true confusion.....
> O, city, full woeful is thine ordinance!

And later:

> This path is stony hard by holy ordinance,
> Which shall take us where we shall be.

Peter tentatively interrupts Jesus when He is wrapped in thought with His despair over Jerusalem and enquires where his Lord will 'keep thy Maundy'. In reply, Jesus reveals that He has a network of supporters by telling Peter that he will see a man 'in simple array, bearing water in the street' and by this simple secret sign he will be led to the house of Simon the Leper.

The action shifts to Jesus approaching Simon's house and again Jesus pauses to reflect in a brief soliloquy that the way ahead will be 'stony'. As Jesus is welcomed by Simon into his house the focus changes yet again another scene in which the High Priests and their co-conspirators move the drama inexorably towards the arrest of Jesus. The constant juxtaposition of scenes of Jesus at the Last Supper with scenes of plotting brings a sense of heightened drama to all His words and deeds. Our first sight of Jesus sitting at His table introduces a curious incident that predates the basis of the novelist Dan Brown's *The Da Vinci Code* by nearly six hundred years. Mary Magdalene enters with a moving soliloquy before she approaches Jesus to anoint His feet with costly ointment and ask for her demons to be cast out. Jesus, having responded with love, authority and tenderness then invites Mary to join them at the table.

The fairly recent discovery of several of the so called 'Gnostic Gospels' at Nag Hamadi, including a *Gospel of Mary Magdalene*, has led to considerable recent interest in the figure of Mary. This has included some speculation that, far from being the harlot that the Church has sometimes portrayed her as she was possibly in a loving or even married relationship with Jesus. We shall re-visit some of these ideas as we explore some of the recent dramatised versions of the life of Jesus but for the moment we can note that the unknown author of the 'N' town cycle of plays offers some support to the view that the feminine-looking figure in Leonardo Da Vinci's painting of the Last Supper may be Mary rather than St. John. This serves as a timely reminder that every age will interpret a play, painting or other work of art according to current cultural trends and understanding.

Judas, having commented on Mary's extravagance, steals away from the table and, standing alone, reflects on his forthcoming betrayal of Jesus. He then goes to the High Priests and organises his sign of betrayal in the form of a kiss and sees the arresting party assembled before he rejoins the disciples at supper. It is by such devices that the dramatist maintains our interest even though this slight variation on the fragmentary and variable shape of the biblical narrative may appear to be artistic licence.

For Christian believers the following section of the play is one of the most sacred, familiar, yet problematic episodes in the entire Passion. Here we see the inauguration of the Communion, Eucharist, or Mass acted out in front of us as if it were happening for the first time in Palestine. Human beings have murdered and hated each other because of their varying interpretations of this event but, freed from much of the ritual and ceremony with which it has been overlaid, the scene of the Last Supper impacts upon its audience with a new freshness. It is possible to see oneself as both witness and participant. Jesus explains simply that in the New Law, He will be the sacrificial lamb and then expounds the mystery whereby the bread will become or represent His body. There is another riveting dramatic moment when Judas takes the bread and Jesus asks him if he is aware of what he has taken. In the ensuing stillness and awkwardness the tension mounts as each disciple in turn pleads that they will not betray their master. Finally Judas leaves with these words ringing in his ears:

Me thou hast sold that was thy friend!
What thou hast begun, bring to an end

And as if to reinforce the extent of Judas' treachery the moment of his exit is followed by the appearance of a demon who gloatingly tells the audience that he is preparing a place for Judas in a stinking hell!

When the action returns to the Last Supper Jesus dominates the stage and, with the exception of a brief interjection from Peter, is the only character to speak until His arrest in Gethsemane. In this sustained monologue He explains the significance of the 'Chalice of the New Testament' and then, in a deeply emotional state, He forecasts His death and resurrection to His uncomprehending disciples. As Peter protests that he will not desert his Master, Jesus is gently tolerant in suggesting that the disciple is out of his depth and points out that he must now rely on Peter to bring comfort to the other disciples because He is now trembling with fear and anticipation at the prospect of what lies ahead. So once again, we see the dramatist providing a more far-reaching insight into the situation than is provided by the economic Gospel narratives. When Jesus leads His followers to another part of the stage that represents Olivet and Gethsemane, He gathers them around for a final monologue in which he explains that He must fulfil prophecy and face death for the sake of sinful humankind. Jesus leaves Peter to keep watch with the others while He goes apart to pray. Once again, Peter is the only other character to speak as he promises to remain vigilant. For actors playing the roles of the remaining disciples the long passages without dialogue provide a huge challenge in focus and concentration.

What ensues is a striking example of the way in which the theatre can tell a story by simple and effective means. Jesus appeals to His heavenly Father:

> O Father, Father! For my sake
> This great passion thou take fro me,
> Which arn ordained that I shall take
> If man's soul saved may be... (etc.)

Even the obscure wording cannot prevent the eight short lines from being intensely moving and providing time for the disciples to fall asleep. When Jesus reprimands His disciples they are unable to reply and, when Jesus returns again after another short prayer to find them sleeping again he looks at them silently with resignation and realises that He is now utterly alone. His third, even more agonised prayer in which He asks to be spared the pain is answered in the Medieval play by the appearance of an angel bearing a chalice. In a symbolic episode the angel administers the elements to Jesus. Thus, Jesus, who in the biblical narrative had asked for the cup to be taken away from him, actually receives and drinks from the cup through the sacred sacrament. At this point the audience as believers may feel that they are present at the communion. The entire compressed drama of Christ's agony in the garden and His dealings with His disciples requires acting of great intensity and many actors participating in these events have testified to their being drained and exhausted by the experience.

Jesus never speaks again at such length in the Passion plays and rarely speaks for more than four short lines at a time until He encounters Mary Magdalene and Thomas after His resurrection. The time of prayer the audience has just witnessed comes to an end with the approach of the arresting party but Jesus, having woken the sleeping disciples now deliberately leads them to meet Judas and his band of knights. The dramatic confrontation that ensues shows Jesus suddenly demonstrating great personal strength of character. He demands to know who it is they seek and when one of them, Leon, says that it is the 'traitor' Jesus of Nazareth whom they know to be present, Jesus tells them simply and directly that they have found Him. The would-be captors fall to the ground in confusion and it is only when Jesus tells them to get up that they recover their composure. Even then, another of the gang repeats the fact that they are looking for Jesus and once again Christ confirms His identity. Finally, Judas steps forward for the fateful kiss and the soldiers arrest Jesus. Throughout these hectic moments we are left with the impression that this is the arrest of no ordinary man and this is confirmed when Peter draws his sword and severs the ear of the High Priest's servant, Malchus. Jesus, in a moment of teaching and healing, rebukes Peter and restores the wretched man's ear: "For he that smites with sword with sword shall be smitten".

As if to cover up their shame in the face of this act of compassion towards His enemies the party then subjects Jesus to a stream of physical and verbal abuse as He is bound with ropes. Bravely, Jesus indignantly tells His tormentors that there was no need to arrest Him like a thief in the night because He had frequently appeared openly to them in the Temple and other public places, preaching, teaching and healing. Unable to withstand Christ's calm logic one of the Priests insists that he is taken away and must not be listened to. The truth is, as always, inconvenient and threatening.

Once Jesus has been led away He is forced to appear before three sets of rulers: all flawed in their own ways: Caiaphas and Annas, the Priests of Israel who find their religious authority threatened; Pilate, the Roman governor of the province who, alone, holds the ultimate power of life and death over the prisoner (so he imagines) and Herod, the petty tyrant, puppet king who was renowned as a character in Medieval drama for his vanity and raving and ranting. In every Passion play of every age it is the clash of these characters with the captive Jesus that provides the nub of the drama. Jesus is unceremoniously shunted between the three authorities and is mocked, insulted, spat upon, flogged and slapped in the face. Even Christ's awareness of Peter's denial of Him does not change the composure and resolute nature of His responses to these encounters and assaults. After numerous accusations of blasphemy and attempting to undermine the law, Jesus, instead of denying that He has claimed to be divine, states simply and powerfully:

> God's Son I am, I say not nay to thee;
> And that ye all shall see at Doomsday,
> When the Son shall come in great power
> and majesty
> And deem the quick and the dead as
> I thee say.

By the time Jesus arrives before Pilate He has been subjected to hideous torture but His only reaction to Pilate's questioning is to reveal that He is untroubled by false accusations and that His main concern is to carry out the purpose of His coming to earth: to save, restore and take mankind to a Heavenly Kingdom. Pilate is baffled by what

Jesus has said and questions Him further about His Kingdom; this disputation brings a note of calm sanity which contrasts sharply with the hysteria of the High Priests.

When Jesus is sent to the buffoon, Herod, He refuses to speak a single word and the more Herod attempts to mock and cajole Jesus the more his frustration mounts. Finally, in a fit of rage he orders Jesus to be flogged, only to intervene in a panic when he realises that he is entirely impotent in the face of Christ's inner strength. Throughout this play we see what Professor Paul Allain in his book on the Suzuki method of acting *The Art of Stillness* has so powerfully described: the sheer potency and theatricality of the total stillness and silence of the actor. During the fifth pageant in the 'N' Town cycle Jesus speaks only once in four short lines; but they are packed with significance because He asserts that Pilate and His accusers would have no power over Him at all were it not given them by His Heavenly Father. He refuses to defend Himself and, as the action progresses to encompass an appearance by Satan, Pilate's wife who has had a prophetic dream, the rabble baying for His death and Pilate's eventually capitulation, He seems totally focussed on the task and ordeal ahead. Jesus is therefore sentenced to die by crucifixion with the criminals Dysmas, who will hang on His right, and Jesmas who will hang on His left. By providing these traditional names for the two condemned men the dramatist has ensured that this is no image removed from reality but an incident of tangible flesh and blood. These names could belong to anyone in a Medieval crowd and could be one of us; they have been used in several of the recently scripted community Passion plays which we shall explore later in this chapter.

Although the unknown author of the York crucifixion play has earned himself the title of 'The York Realist' for the uncompromising physical detail of his play, the writer of the 'N' Town cycle is hardly less bold. His play begins with Jesus being driven towards His death carrying His cross; an incident that lies at the heart of many re-enactments of the Passion. He is witnessed by a number of sympathetic women who lament the injustice of the situation, providing an 'on-stage' audience for the events and representing us. Jesus

The Jesus Of The Passions

now breaks His long silence and in an eloquent and selfless speech tells the women and us not to weep for Him but for their own world and the misfortunes that may come upon them.

Jesus does not speak again until He is hanging from the upright cross. The audience has witnessed the cruel stretching of Jesus to fit the cross, the driving in of nails, the effort of the soldiers in bringing the cross into an upright position and dropping it into its mortise in order for it to remain steady. All this demands very considerable skill and ingenuity in the construction of the cross to enable the actors playing the soldiers/torturers to heave on ropes and drive in the nails and the actor playing Jesus to come to no physical harm while he is apparently hanging from the cross. Whatever physical solutions to these problems are found they inevitably involve considerable effort and discomfort and great skill on the part of the actors.

When this translation of the play was first performed in the city-centre grounds of Birmingham Cathedral, England in the late 1990s, the setting up of the cross coincided with the evening throng attending the bars and nightclubs. A bemused section of the population walked close by the scene of the crucifixion and it was difficult not to hear in their mockery and obvious embarrassment the same voices that must have been heard at the original Golgotha. The crucifixion had become a public statement.

When Mary the mother of Jesus first enters the scene to lament the fate of her son Jesus appears not to hear her. Instead, He prays for forgiveness for the Jews. His repetition of the words "forgive them" not only gives them added force for the audience but, contrary to some of the publicity that has surrounded the performance of Passion Plays in Oberammergau and elsewhere, there is a clear indication that the Jews must be absolved from any guilt surrounding the death of Jesus. The torturers are joined by Jesmas in mocking Jesus for His claim to be God's Son but Dysmas rebukes him, comparing their wrongs with the blameless life of Jesus. Then he pleads:

> Now mercy, good Lord, mercy,
> and forget me not

When thou comest to thy kingdom
and to thy bliss.

And Jesus grants him his request :

This same day in paradise
With me, thy God, thou shalt there be.

Mary wonders if she has offended her son because it seems
He has spoken to everyone present except her but Jesus
then turns His attention to her. Firstly He ensures that John
understands that he must take care of her but then He
points out to Mary that she already understands the
necessity of His death: to pay Adam's ransom and restore
mankind to 'bliss'. 'Why' He asks, should she be displeased
when His death has pleased His Father? Not for the first
time, perhaps, Jesus' treatment of His mother appears
rather harsh but for Medieval Christians the doctrinal
certainties must over-ride the human situation, and at this
point Mary embraces the cross, the central symbol of the
faith.

The crucifixion section of virtually every Passion Play
ever written is structured around what are traditionally
known as Jesus' 'seven last words from the cross'. These, of
course, are seven statements rather than single words all
provided by the Gospels. Whereas we are given very clear
indications of the words of Jesus the Gospels give us the
barest of indications of what is said by the other characters or
indeed, who they are. Therefore much of the dialogue and
some of the characters in the Passion Plays are invented.

However, the words of Jesus have an incredible power
and none more so that when He appears to experience a
crisis in which, though He is both God and Man, the man
takes over. Firstly he cries out that He is thirsty and when He
has taken the vinegar handed up to Him on a sponge He
reaches His bleakest moment. In order to make this utterly
personal the writers of the Gospels and the dramatists of the
Mystery Plays have Jesus speaking in His native tongue; Eli
Eli, lamasabachthani! This desperate cry is translated in the
Gospels as, "My God, my God, why hast thou forsaken me?"
and in order that the audience of the plays may understand
the dramatists have found various ways of providing a trans-

lation within the dialogue. The 'N' Town writer expands the speech as follows:

> Eli, Eli, lamasabachthani?
> My father in heaven on high,
> Why dost thou me forsake?
> The frailty of my mankind,
> With mickle (much) strength it
> 'ginneth to pain!
> Ha, dear Father, have me in mind,
> And let death my sorrow slake. (quench)

Similarly Maurice Hussey renders the Chester Passion play as:

> Eli, eli, eli, eli!
> My God my God, I speak to thee!
> Eli, lama sabachthani?
> Why hast thou forsaken me?

Here, the playwright has cleverly woven the English translation into the text.

In all versions the desolate cry of Jesus is met with mockery and then He speaks His final words. As if to emphasise to the Medieval audience that it is the Catholic Church that teaches and expounds the faith, Jesus utters His dying words in Latin. This was a powerful means of emphasising that what the spectators were witnessing was central to what went on in their church. For many modern audiences this is no longer the case and many directors have replaced the Latin with familiar English words.

Strictly speaking, Christ's Passion is now at an end but the story does not end there and, indeed, there is a good deal of evidence to suggest that the first dramas in the Catholic tradition had their origins in Easter celebrations. Many Passion Plays devote very little time to the Resurrection but those that do often include non-scriptural episodes that illustrate the potency of Christ's redeeming work. The most extensive of these are the 'Harrowing of Hell' plays in which the spirit of Jesus descends to hell to rout the Devil and rescue captive Adam. Such plays add little to our appreciation of Jesus as a character but do provide some spectacular and gripping action.

It is with the various appearances of the risen Christ that all the Medieval Passion plays give a series of striking images of Jesus. Firstly in the moving encounter with Mary Magdalene in the garden, a scene of great delicacy and restraint that complements Mary's earlier entrance at the Last Supper and secondly in Jesus' meeting along the way to Emmaus with two of the disciples. When he was making the adaptation of the 'N' Town plays for Birmingham Douglas Sugano chose to omit this play because it is excessively wordy for a modern production, and thus it is not mentioned in the Banns we have explored. However, this play is worthy of some attention as it unique to 'N' Town and shows Jesus exhibiting great compassion for the two bereft disciples as He walks with them unrecognised, and provides a technical challenge to the director in His sudden disappearance from the table once He has broken bread with them. The third incident that features in the Passion plays is the appearance of Jesus to the disciples after Thomas has expressed his doubts that some of their company have seen the risen Lord. The moment when Jesus enters and asks Thomas to place his hands on His wounds is one of the most memorable encounters between two characters in the entire drama, and from that moment of intimacy and personal declaration of belief and faith the plays expand into Christ's ascension.

By contrast with the quiet, intimate encounters the scene of the ascension in all the Medieval Passion Plays is expansive and full of high ceremony. Jesus takes His leave of His disciples with words of encouragement and inspiration but the focus eventually shifts to us all. Wakefield in Gordon Honeycombe's version is fairly typical. After a long speech in which He explains the work He has achieved, Jesus concludes:

> My love never has denied thee,
> That thou must have known.
> But now I yearn that some return
> Of love to me be shown;
> I ask thy love, but that thing,
> And that you strive to flee from sin,
> And live in charity with men.
> Then in my bliss

Thou shalt remain
Always.

One by one the people in the crowd lift their hands to the risen Christ crying "Te Deum laudamus" until the whole multitude stands worshipping, crying out "Te Deum laudamus" and the place fills with light. Then in silence the company departs, and the light fades until only the figure of Christ is seen with His arms outstretched before Him"

Other plays end with choruses of angels and the appearance of God receiving His Son in heaven; in some plays we see Jesus discoursing with the angels and telling of the work He has done. Perhaps the most inspirational ending is the simplicity of the words of the Chester plays that were also used in the twentieth-century productions in Canterbury Cathedral. Jesus says:

My sweet brethren, beloved and dear,
To me is granted full power,
In heaven and earth, far and near,
For my godhead is most.
To teach all men now go ye,
That in the world will followed be,
In the name of the Father and me,
And of the Holy Ghost.

Passions as tourist attractions

The Medieval Passion Plays have continued to inspire performances and adaptations in many parts of the world. In 1997 the Royal Shakespeare Company commissioned a version by Edward Kemp who drew not only on the cycle plays but on the Gnostic Gospels and the Tyndale edtion of the Bible to create a text to be directed by Katie Mitchell. This work led to extensive discussion with the actors that is fascinatingly outlined in the edition published by Nick Hern.

Probably by far the best known Passion Play is that which is performed every ten years in the Austrian village of Oberammergau and which has now become a major international tourist attraction. The play was first performed in 1633 when the villagers made a vow to celebrate their salvation from death at the time of the plague by remembering Christ's suffering in the form of a Passion Play. They have kept their vow to present the play every ten years since and were initially able to draw upon rich tradition of religious folk plays already popular throughout Bavaria and Swabia.

The earliest productions of the play were staged in the church or churchyard, but the construction of a railway link with Munich and growing interest in the play contributed to making it a tourist attraction and a number of permanent stages were built. The present theatre dates from the 1930s and reflects the somewhat gothic style of the current text and production style. The text appears to have originated in mid fifteenth-century Augsburg and was rewritten in the 1750s. In 1810 a new text was created by Fr. Ottmar Weiss and some of this remains in use today. However, a further adaptation by Fr. Alois Daisenberger in 1850 and continuous minor changes have all contributed to the present script and this has been much supported by the composition of a number of elaborate musical scores. As Dr. Franz Dietl points out in his introduction to the English translation to the text of 1990, the play has acquired an almost classical form. The incidents in the Passion of Jesus are shown in 14 acts, each separated by comments from the Prologue and Chorus and interspersed with scenes from the Old Testament that illustrate and prefigure the theological significance of the events. In many ways, therefore, the play resembles one of the great Bach Passions where the emphasis lies on the listeners meditating on the meaning of what is seen and heard.

Oberammergau's Passion Play operates on a gigantic scale. It involves a huge cast of local people and close to one hundred performances, each of which occupies a significant proportion of a day. The role of Jesus is now usually undertaken by two actors after much speculation and competition amongst the local people and this undertaking is seen by the organisers as a sacred act of personal worship and commitment.

Jesus is shown as a combination of pictures from all four gospels and the emphasis is on His recorded words and deeds, starting with His 'cleansing of the Temple' and culminating (very briefly) in His resurrection. In contrast, the various writers have provided substantial, imaginative parts

The Jesus Of The Passions

for Peter and Judas and through a series of mono-
logues/soliloquies these characters reflect on their inner
struggles and failures in relation to their Master. Whereas
Jesus speaks many familiar lines taken directly from the
Gospels other characters have fresh and sometimes
powerful dialogue.

Some critics have argued that the sheer spectacle of
Oberammergau brings it closer to Hollywood than to the
profound allegory of some of the Mystery Plays, but for
many the production is a deeply moving experience that
gains from the obvious absorption and devotion of the community participants.

Passions in the Modern Church

The tradition of staging Passion Plays has continued
virtually unbroken in many predominantly Catholic
countries and even in such countries as Poland that were
under communist rule after the Second World War there has
been a considerable resurgence of interest in the plays.
However, it is in the largely English-Speaking Protestant
Churches in the USA and the British Isles that the most
substantial explosion of productions of Passion Plays has
taken place in the last three decades. We have already seen
that British cities with their own cycles of Mystery Plays had
revived their traditions but an even more powerful,
evangelical movement has taken the idea of the Passion Play
and made it their own. Passion Plays are now performed in
many North American communities and seem to vie with
each other for their sheer size and spectacle. One of the
most notable of these productions is staged at the Crystal
Cathedral in California with an audience of 2,500 and seen
by millions of additional people through the medium of
television. The publicity for this play, *The Glory of Easter*
reads more like a blurb for *Peter Pan* as a spectacular
pantomime than for a play about Jesus. "Six angels fly
throughout the production, some fly as high as 80
feet...animals play an integral part: Donkey, five horses,
water buffalo, baby camel, peacocks, sheep and goats". The
stage itself is said to be, "one of the largest in the world" and
a cast of 100, with professional actors in the lead roles is

accompanied by the music of the London Symphony and Seattle Symphony Orchestras.

This is no longer the robust, intimate world of the Mystery Plays nor the high, meditative seriousness of Oberammergau, this is modern technological mankind with special effects including earthquakes, thunder and lightning, compacting the story into 90 minutes of breathtaking spectacle. The text, a modernised paraphrase of scripture by Paul David Dunn, who also directs the show, as it inevitably must be called, provides a rather sanitised Jesus who according to a trenchant criticism of the production by Michael Linton is, "kind and wise. He heals. He makes people happy by loving them and telling them that they can have anything they want if they only believe".

One of the most significant differences between the *Glory of Easter* and other Passions is that it appears merely to allow the audience to remain as impartial spectators. Even the crowd, does not actually bay for the blood of Jesus and sees Him condemned to death in silence. At no stage is the audience challenged with the idea that they are part of the sinful world which crucified Jesus and, as Linton points out, the concept of the Atonement is totally absent.

In some senses the setting of the Crystal Cathedral and other similar fixed venues militates against the ability of the Jesus of the Passions to challenge us. Inevitably, the distant figure is seen more as a character in movie with a stunning setting and, even if technology allows a 'close up', this lacks the immediacy of an actor on a rough wooden platform establishing eye contact with those gathered around. Furthermore, any permanent staging that is artificially removed from more earthy surroundings has the effect of distancing the subject matter from the real lives of ordinary people.

Passions in the Community: walking with Jesus

For the reasons we have just examined some of the most remarkable Passions in recent years have been staged in what have come to be known as 'found spaces', that is non-theatrical venues that simply lend themselves to performance. The small Herefordshire town of Leominster in the UK, for example, now mounts a Passion Play every four years and this is staged at a variety of locations around the town. The audience follows the action quite literally and gathers around a series of spaces to see the events enacted. The use of technology is virtually non-existent and the cast of local amateurs is professionally directed. Significantly, the production has its origin and driving force in no particular church nor does it claim any specified denominational allegiance. This has increasingly been the tendency, and the website of 'Passions UK' lists Passion Play productions in a considerable number of British towns and cities. Together with offering guidance for communities seeking to mount their own plays the website also advertises the need for volunteers to take part in already established productions: indeed, it would now be possible for enthusiasts to be involved in Passion Plays somewhere every year!

Typical of this new movement are some of the most innovative and influential of recent productions of the *Passion* which take place on the Wintershall Estate in Surrey. These productions are part of the vision of the Estate's owners, Peter and Ann Hutley, who have established a Charitable Trust with the purpose of using drama as a means of spreading the Christian faith through "thrilling pieces of theatre". One-time Buddhist and soldier, Peter Hutley was profoundly influenced by the reported apparitions of the Virgin Mary and subsequent events in the Bosnia-Herzegovinan village of Medjugorje in the 1981, and by its charismatic parish priest Father Jozo Zovko, "the man who I believed was more like Jesus than any man I had ever seen or would ever see – humorous, stern, interesting, emotional" and who was imprisoned by the State Police. Embracing the Roman Catholic faith and moved by his acquisition of a piece of land on which an historic barn is situated, Peter Hutley determined to "do something for God" and, initially using his neighbours and members of his family, created a Nativity play employing extracts from Eliot's *Journey of the Magi* and some biblical text.

Thus, the plays had a relatively modest origin with a Nativity in a barn but soon this had developed into its current scale involving horses, cows, camels, donkeys and a large cast playing to audiences of many hundreds. The play commences as darkness begins to fall and the gathered members of the audience, who have been consuming hot food and drink served from an outside caravan, see Mary and Joseph approaching over the brow of a hill on a donkey before they are ushered into the barn where animals are stalled. The smells, sights and sounds integrate to form a piece of total theatre. As the play progresses in its present form, now scripted entirely from the New International Version of the Bible, it takes on some of the characteristics of the Medieval Mystery plays: Herod is transformed into the Devil who does battle with the Archangel Michael and is finally hurled into the pit of Hell. The actor who suffers this fate is, in fact a local Baptist minister!

Emboldened by the success of the Nativity Peter Hutley scripted a *Passion* for performance in the grounds of the estate and then, in response to the Pope's call for action at the Millennium, created an even more massive *Life of Christ*, for, as this remarkable entrepreneur remarked to me, "without Christ there would be no millennium"! This production now involves a cast of some two hundred actors drawn from the local community and is directed by Ashley Herman with such professional actors as James Burke-Dunsmore in the role of Jesus. As with many such productions, the commitment required of the amateur cast is enormous and many regard the one week run of the play as part of their holiday. They are supported by highly sophisticated theatre technology and the performances involve the audience of three thousand moving between various locations for a period of six hours. Highly effective use is made of two lakes and a variety of hillsides, structures and pastures. The biblical figure of Luke, the writer of one of the gospels, acts as a chorus/narrator figure and, for example, following the enactment of the 'feeding of the five thousand' by the lakeside, suggests to the audience that it is time for them to eat too! It is the experience of mingling with the cast and the characters that gives the Wintershall plays a quality that so often emanates from 'promenade' productions such as those of the *Mysteries* at the National

Theatre and Canterbury Cathedral. As Peter Hutley put it to me "the audience is walking with Jesus".

His scripts, all based on the New International Version, follow the biblical narrative closely and have provided a platform for others who wish to mount similar productions. The energy and enterprise generated by his productions have resulted in his obtaining permission to stage the *Passion* in *Trafalgar Square in 2010*.

The organisation of Wintershall now offers a trilogy of plays: *The Acts of the Apostles*, *The Wintershall Nativity* and *The Life of Christ* which are unashamedly marketed as, "three plays that could change your life". Indeed, the many audience tributes and appreciations I have been able to read testify to the transformative and inspirational power of the productions: one simply stated, "to have Jesus Christ thrust into my imagination so powerfully....by means of live drama is a new and exciting experience that I wish to share with others".

All the Wintershall productions are spectacular and detailed: they are marketed with the confidence of a professional theatrical commodity, they have their attendant merchandise and place great emphasis on what many would consider to be biblical 'authenticity' in terms of costume, language and historical accuracy. In some respects Wintershall is like a Greek Easter where the lamb is the symbol of the approaching sacrifice and appears on greetings in supermarkets and butchers shops, for the website advertising of the *Wintershall Passion* sits alongside their advertisement for organic lamb. However, many of the cast clearly approach their involvement with a deep sense of evangelising zeal and for many members of the audience, the biblical events are brought to life in an extraordinary way.

As a direct result of the inspiration of Peter Hutley and his daughter Charlotte de Klee, Suzanne Lofthus, the director of the Edinburgh-based Cutting Edge Theatre Productions directed an open air Passion Play, working with a large cast to create a production for the Scottish town of Auchtermuchty in the year 2000. Such was the success of this production, seen initially by a thousand people, that it was decided to repeat it and to consider whether it might become an annual event. However, Sir Jack Stewart Clark from Dundas Castle, who had seen the Wintershall plays, was so motivated and moved by the experience that he suggested his estate as a suitable venue for a similar venture. Suzanne Lofthus, who openly professed her Christian faith, was sufficiently convinced by the possibilities of this Scottish 'found space' with its loch, walls and garden tomb, that she agreed to undertake a production using Hutley's script. This five-year project then expanded into a production in Glasgow for which the Wintershall script was also used.

Perhaps the most significant moment in this off-shoot from Wintershall, however, was the creation of a new script by the screenwriter Kamala Maniam for an Edinburgh 'Easter Play'. Using the gospels as her basic source she wrote what was in essence a 'traditional' play; but a more recent development has been her response to a request to construct a text in which Mary Magdalene, Zacchaeus and Nicodemus appear as contemporary characters. Building on this move away from historical 'authenticity', the organisers of the Glasgow play for 2011 have approached a non-Christian playwright because, in the words of the director, "we get a modern and relevant script".

We might speculate as to the various conflicting issues that arise during the continuing creation of 'Passion Plays'. Certainly they appear to have gained a new impetus from within the Christian community, albeit initially based in the relatively affluent commuter belt of South East England and staged in privately owned estates. Even though their purpose appears to be overtly evangelical and that the website set up by Suzanne Lofthus as a result of her experience encourages communities to stage Passion Plays as a means of Christian witness and education it is, perhaps, revealing that in order to obtain a script that is 'modern and relevant' it was necessary to turn to a non-Christian. It is certainly possible for Passion Plays to be swamped by piety and there is something raw and stimulating about engaging a cast and audience who are not believers with the drama of the Passion. The Mysteries that originated in Canterbury but expanded to Dartford, Birmingham, Malvern and

Tewkesbury used leading actors from the TV shows *Blue Peter* and *Neighbours* as Jesus together with a well-known comedian as God. None of these actors and very few of the large local casts were drawn from the church community and, even though the then Archbishop of Canterbury wrote to the director saying that the production, "did more than any number of sermons" the focus remained throughout on the innate drama and human emotions of live theatre.

Perhaps, as Suzanne Lofthus puts it, "Theatre is still being used to communicate the Gospel as it started out" but also adds, "Theatre and Christianity in harmony - now that's rare!"

CHAPTER FOUR

Jesus In The Contemporary Theatre: Jesus Rocks

This chapter concerns itself with the story of how the Christian churches almost lost Jesus.

It will especially focus on the biggest Jesus moment on stage that dwarfs all else. This is the Andrew Lloyd-Webber-Tim Rice production of *Jesus Christ Superstar*. This extraordinary work, and its off-stage machinations, dominate any general consideration of Jesus and the modern stage musical. As my co-writer has mentioned in an earlier chapter it heralds something dramatically new in western theatre. In more recent time it has been the forerunner of musicals adapted for rock and pop culturally attuned generations. Within that context it has become the unintended financial saviour of London's West End.

The initial New York production provided for all time one of the most extravagant and 'over the top' stage sets. There were also costumes belonging to fantasy world, extravagant in cost, incredible in design, and in themselves works of art. Some came for these two things. It suggested pyrotechnics could make text and actor 'also – rans'.

JCS heralded in brutal reality that the stuffing had been knocked out of reverence. While toiling South Americans were calling on Jesus the Liberator to aid their freedom from corrupt regimes and horrendous inequality in living standards and expectations, *JCS* for Western audiences meant a desire to see Jesus top the record charts and become another consumer item. For a while he was claimed by commercialism and many a Christian and church would be wowed by the thought that the name of Jesus was hung in Broadway and London's Cambridge Circus. They would dutifully come and worship the new born pop star. *Time* magazine described the phenomenon as the 'Gold Rush to Golgotha.'

However before embarking on the *JCS* trail there must first be a general look at other texts that brought Jesus centre stage, as well as describing various social and religious happenings of the late 1960s. *JCS* did not arrive as it were from nowhere. It was a controversial show and it was not without attention from loonies. Of course some would say that at times the production stretched sanity.

My co-writer has already explored the complicated world of the stage and censorship, but a few further comments would seem useful before approaching not only the world of *JCS* but of other less known but flamboyant religious musicals and texts where Jesus is seen as a pop star, or gay, or transsexual, a woman, even simply mad. There again, he could be all of those things at one and the same time. At very least he is seen as another reasonable sort of person willing to 'tell all' once trapped in the seeming decadent world of the *Jerry Springer Show* and the stage offshoot *Jerry Springer – The Opera* where people are happy to be in a public confessional.

Unfortunately for any playwright the effete Aryan of white Sunday school art dominates the thinking of many, not that, as *Time* magazine once pointed out, the image is hardly more subjective than the contemporary Black Jesus in a dashiki.

To recapitulate briefly: after the sixteenth century Reformation, through decades and centuries, it was not permissible to represent Jesus, Satan or God on stage until the late 1960s. That the various religious elements, and non-believers sharing similar sentiments, but from different perspectives, achieved this blanket censorship is nothing short of the extraordinary, some might say, ridiculous. It must stand as one of the most remarkable power games in religious history, let alone general British history, and certainly in the history of theatre.

It does of course reflect on the power wielded at one time by the Church, and principally the state Church in Britain. Archbishops and bishops could pronounce on seemingly everything, and did so, even if their knowledge was limited, as was the case with Archbishop Lang, for, according to his chaplain, His Grace had seen but six films in his whole life. It did not stop him from wishing to ensure the cinema of the 1930s exercised a good moral influence.

It is almost comical to realise that along the way came the removal of the ban that ministers of religion should not be portrayed as comic characters or villains, when some of them are painfully just that. At least in 1945 Philip King's farce on the clergy *See How They Run* made the London West End, to be revived with success at London's Duchess Theatre in the summer of 2006, where its slick routines caused much hilarity. It was vintage comedy. *The Church Times* in their review printed July1, 2006, lovingly headlined "Arrest Most of these Vicars."

The stage has not been alone in suffering censorship. At one time in the 20th century the cinema and wireless vied as the most popular forms of entertainment. The two were carefully monitored to ensure an educative power was present, that general moral values were upheld. The Cinema Christian Council worried that films showed shootings, murders, fighting, thefts and the murky underworld. In the late 1930s a code issued by American film producers, approved by the British Board of Film Censors said their work would uphold the sanctity of marriage, not justify adultery; ban obscenity, undue exposure, pointed profanity and any reference to 'sexual perversion.' As with many things of this nature sentiments are fine, but they seldom last long.

Underlying the tension is the belief of playwrights, producers, directors and actors that there is an intrinsic right to say and do, although even the most forceful proponents might object to certain subjects. Theirs is the right to challenge prevailing notions, especially those that seem destructive or foisted upon the public by self-appointed grandees of public life. In this they do not claim special privileges, for I've no reason to think otherwise than they would wish free speech for everyone, but in the nature of their discipline there is no compromise.

The virtual demise of censorship has led to the emergence of those who have taken it upon themselves to either form associations or bring together groups of the like-minded. Obviously theatre affects only a tiny minority compared with the major forms of communication, but it does possess advantages for protestors. Theatre protests make news, for their patch can be located quickly and pictures of production hoardings and gathered crowds look good on a newspaper page or television screen. Protestors can also make in-roads into besieging actors by the stage doors, and indeed this strategy was employed at venues staging *Jerry Springer – The Opera*, and where even serving staff were subject to abuse.

It has not been easy to suss whether the rows and rows of protestors outside theatres, for instance protesting against *Jerry Springer – The Opera* represent anything more than a minority, and sometimes a travelling minority. Certainly these groups have not been without success. The first proposed *Springer* tour was truncated, and finally abandoned, when some theatres bowed to the shouts of the appalled who probably had never read the text, or watched the television show.

The ever growing power of the media and the continual widening sphere of communicatory forms has enabled 'protest' groups to reach a far wider public in a shorter space of time, and organise themselves to greater affect. In the 21st century one searing article in the major circulation *Daily Mail* can influence public and media opinion and cause the 'alert' signal for those monitoring public performance. Again a theatre reviewer and the printed review can decide on whether a play succeeds or fails. It is said that the Englishman Clive Barnes, who forged a mighty review power base in New York, could end the life a new play in days, if he found the production lacking. A collection of indifferent reviews can achieve a negative effect, as arguably with the 2009 English National Opera production of *Messiah* and directed by one of the major names of current English theatre, Deborah Warner.

On a general level, the playwright venturing into a religious area soon finds there are contemporary Christians who while unsure whether Jesus should be in some way represented on stage do have another stricture. They show the red light to anyone who would put into modern speech the words of Jesus, usually meaning those found in the King James 1611 version. They do not accept that anyone should play the role of Jesus. They see this as sacrilegious. Should they allow some form of representation then they will judge this on a number of often spurious grounds, one of which asks whether the person playing Jesus is a committed Christian. They cannot see and hear first, and then decide how valid the question might be. At the same time they have their own idea of Jesus and even in verbalising these impressions they begin to create some kind of drama, not that this would be acknowledged by them.

It reminds me of my first stage play *Feel The Spirit*, the story of the 19th century revival pair of Moody and Sankey. One of the actresses was singled out for her passion, fervour and undeniable love of the Lord. Unfortunately she was the non-Christian in the cast. The person who mistakenly identified the true believer could have taken away at least a positive – that the actress imagined Christians are joyous people, a change from the oft held image of a dour unbending set of joyless people.

Others will dismiss any playing of Jesus in a modern setting, and one that could see Jesus wearing shall we say, a pair of jeans, or minus beard and long hair. In one sense it is not surprising such groups exist, for if I do not generalise too much, it seems to have been the case that some religious people have assumed that any new form of communication or one with mass appeal should first pass through their sieve. Stage and film, radio and television, less so the newspaper, have been seen as avenues for the Faith to be disseminated, and at very least never to allow religious matters to be seen in a bad light.

Certainly up to the end of the Second World War Christians exercised their own form of censorship, or at least were consulted by those who would not wish to advance their ideas beyond the stage of no return, and then incur a dreaded protest.

There also exists a strange breed of person who may not go to church, other than perhaps at a major festival, or in a village area on Feast Sunday before galloping off with the hounds. That said he or she may ring the church bells but not stay to service but they see Jesus as theirs. More so, in their view, this Jesus, as played on any stage should represent western values or be the kind of Jesus that was most popular when Brittania ruled the waves. It is the Jesus of Percy Dearmer's hymn, 'Jesus, good above all other/ Gentle child of gentle mother/ In a stable born our brother.' It is a Jesus who will not give offence. This is the Jesus who half-smiles benevolently from paintings that hang from the walls of church vestries and runs counter to the Che Guevara look-alike poster that adorns the bedroom walls of radical politically motivated Christians.

All this said and done there are always reasonable grounds for objection. There should never be a blank cheque. Where there is no intellectual enquiry, and fear - bound religiosity exists, truth invariably suffers, and to some degree this is the subject of *Inherit The Wind*, a play from 1935, filmed in 1960, revived in 1992 with Stephen Daldry directing, and with Trevor Nunn assuming that role at the Old Vic London, December 2008. It gained much from having Kevin Spacey gaining the plum role of Drummond. The play text was dated and a depiction of Christians in smug, self-righteous mode became somewhat boring. Nevertheless, it was interesting.

A play's text may deserve harsh words, or a writer deliberately sets out to ridicule what is seen by many as sacred and fails miserably. The text may reveal poor research, or the direction of the play sucks, and perish the thought the acting is vapid. No company likes to see a headline such as "A dead-pan waste of talent" as run part-way across a page in the *London Evening Standard* of Monday, August 6, 2007, for Robert Dawson-Scott's review of *Night Time* at the Traverse, Edinburgh.

Unfortunately raw, often naked emotion runs riot in sometimes disturbing fashion. This chapter cannot avoid calling in upon these stereotypes.

Regrettably those who do not feel strongly one way or the other, or even have appreciated some of the religious insights of writers such as Brenton, Berkoff and Dennis Potter, do not usually form themselves into what might be called an 'approval' group; who wave banners, organise petitions, flood emails or faxes to the desired source.

Yet, as shown elsewhere in this book hostilities can be traced back to the mind-set that followed Reformation. It also has to be said that the Protestant wing of the Church has been the more vociferous. The more Catholic tradition expresses the body of faith in the works of the imagination.

As Tom F. Driver says in Finley Eversole's edited *Christian Faith and the Contemporary Arts*, Protestantism has at "its centre the principle of protest, the arts function primarily as celebration." Driver posits the thought that the contemporary Protestant dramatist faces a world that is basically secular. "Even when he confronts an audience of churchgoers, most often he confronts persons whose awareness of the great Christian tradition is vague. He must therefore teach them the law in the same breath that he proclaims to them freedom from the law. He must make them religious and redeem them from religiosity in the same moment. In short, he must speak with a Yes and a No, he must, as they say, become dialectical."

Driver finds only one good contemporary Christian play, which seems to fulfil this requirement and this is Gunter Rutenborn's *The Sign of Jonah*. His text dates from 1957, revised by 1962. I am at a loss to provide an example in 2010 that has the genuinely Protestant dialectic throughout, and in terms of this book where Jesus takes centre stage, and where He is not a vehicle for a playwright to labour a particular cause.

Many of the factors thus far that have been mentioned make their appearance in this extraordinary story of *Jesus Christ Superstar* from Andrew Lloyd-Webber and Tim Rice. However as I have made in earlier allusion, the duo and their *JCS* were not the only musical playwrights post 1955 utilising religion and ultimately interpreting in some way either the imagined Messiah or Jesus. Before them, the infamous Sixties spawned a number of interesting works.

The successes of these in their varied style and direction, and more so monetary success, must surely have set many a producer's mind into thinking mould. There was at the time an extraordinary Church based production *A Man Dies* which is described and discussed in another chapter, and not at this juncture because it did not make a West End stage, outside of the Royal Albert Hall, London, which gives space to all kinds of art forms.

The Marvin-HooperHooper piece did make television screens, and may well have encouraged thinking on mounting something specifically Christian but which would be seen as 'theatre' irrespective of any underlying thrust. Part answer came in the early 1960s. In terms of sympathetic Christian based text there is little that can compare on the general theatre stage with the musical *Black Nativity* that I might have seen six or more times, and each time adored.

It was a re-telling of the classic nativity story with an entirely black cast and that in itself was something fairly sensational at the time. Originally written by the celebrated writer Langston Hughes, and first performed on Broadway, December 11, 1961, it comprised traditional Christmas carols sung in gospel style with the bonus of several songs specifically written for the show.

The original American production saw an initially darkened theatre with barefoot singers clad only in white robes and carrying electric candles walk on stage an singing the popular Christmas lyric version to' Go Tell It on the Mountain'. The stage at first bathed in orange and blue lights becomes bathed in a deep red hue. Mary's contractions are felt by the use of African drums and percussion.

The central text is based on the Lucan narratives dealing with the announcement and birth of Jesus. To this is added verse, singing and dance. One critic wrote, "His tone has that intimate, elusive, near-tragic, near-comic sound of the Negro blues, and is equally defiant of analysis." Black Nativity speaks of the Jesus to be, the prophesied one of Isaiah 9, of the 'Magnificat' and other interpretative stresses of Langston Hughes. In a sense *Black Nativity* and the *JCS* of the next decade are like chalk and cheese but essentially in stage terms the former shows the power of drama that does not need all the paraphernalia of the latter and which I shall describe in some detail later in this chapter.

Fiddler on the Roof (1964) based on stories by Shalom Aleichem, *(Tenye and his Daughters)* about life in the Jewish 'schtels', or settlements, in Tsarist Russia 1905, pleases many Jewish people, but not all, for the latter see it giving a distorted view of Judaism, but it makes for amusing, informative, and sometimes inspirational and moving viewing. Ian Bradley in his excellent book *You've Gotta Have A Dream* refers to an untitled song about the long awaited Messiah that was cut during its pre-Broadway run. He remarks, "The Messiah envisaged here is equally far from the angst-ridden figure of *Jesus Christ Superstar* and the stern unmovable judge of *Carousel.*" The production is constantly given new life with one of its revivals at London's Savoy Theatre in 2007. *The Methodist Recorder's* editor Moira Sleight noted both the fact that the spiritual side of life was central to the characters and that the people displayed a real sense of the resilience of the human spirit. The story focuses on a community of Jews trying to preserve their traditional way of life in difficult and unfriendly circumstances. In one of the London runs the baker was played by an actor with the surname of Bacon.

Man of La Mancha (1965) had a personal mission statement. The song lyric for 'To Dream the Impossible Dream' brings us close to the Gospel's description of the crucified Jesus. The show *Sweet Charity* (1966) is set in a basement garage where the church meets, and the song listing contains the powerful Rhythm of Life. Gospel choirs, church choirs and male voice choirs have made the song their own in times since.

Both those shows may have had plenty of religion dotted about them, as indeed from a Jewish perspective did the ever popular *Fiddler on the Roof*, but they did not attract protest. Yet a few years later one surmises that some of the sermon spoken by the character John Sebastian Brubeck would have brought out the protestors from their firesides, for street lingo of the time is used, as with 'thou shalt dig thy neighbour.' And they may have objected to the Pelagian refrain 'Clip your wings and fly high. You can do it if you try.' Still, others would agree with the latter critique.

To many it was Stephen Sondheim's, *Company* (1970) that broke the traditional musical score mould established by people such as Rodgers and Hammerstein. We were transported into the realism of life, at least the style of the upper middle class, who are seen as spiritually empty or as the New York paper *Village Voice* expressed most delicately, "In *Company* no one dreams, only survives." However this was not ear-filling, mind–blowing, eye-batting, bustling material that Malachi Martin says lifts you right to the pitch of yourself.

Hence, for a rock generation who were by now into a host of popular best selling bands such as *Jefferson Airplane*, *Doors*, *Rolling Stones* and *Led Zeppelin* something more was demanded. Into the apparent gap came two young guys. No-one thought of ringing the weekly music papers to gain column inches on Sondheim's *Company*. They knew the answer would be negative, but that was about to change and somehow Jesus was mixed up in it all. Jesus would be a modern Superstar.

Jesus Christ Superstar arrived shortly after apoplexy had permeated the ranks of some Christian organizations. Two productions contributed to this, and for some people confirmed their view that theatre is of the anti-christ.

The late 1960s and early '70s saw the musical *Hair*. The letter columns of the religious press were filled with angry and vehement denunciations of the lifestyle portrayed in this lively and engaging theatrical piece. The production contained an enticing mix of profane language, nudity, sexual simulation and a disregard for the very moral fabric of society. It also contained numerous Christian references. For a heady mix *Hair* could move from hallucinogenic drugs to precious words from the Lord's Supper, "This is the body and blood of Jesus Christ."

It was also the case that many Christians had been shaken to the core by the action of the Dean of St Paul's London, who had invited the cast on its third birthday to take part in a religious service in those august surroundings. Objectors saw it as the Church applauding the very things mentioned in the last paragraph, an open-arms invitation to immorality.

In some respects it was 'part and parcel' of 'trendy' happenings in the Church, not that sexual adventuring was yet present, that would occur in the 1990s in Sheffield. Beat music had invaded churches; although it was not seen by some to possess any intrinsic value, it was the case that it brought young people into sacred confines where they might hear the message.

For some it was all going astray, and a potent mix of *Hair* and St. Paul's was enough to light the fuse paper; protest followed. The *Hair* cast, and some its music, found themselves in New York's Manhattan Episcopal Cathedral of St John on the occasion of the production's third anniversary. The nudity scenes were missing, although it was noted that braless girls leaned languorously against the pews, with bright balloons announcing to the less conversant that "God is Love."

As *Time Magazine* reported May 24, 1971, the Hair numbers were intended to be only a framework for a *Mass in F* written by *Hair* composer Galt MacDermot. Star theologian Harvey Cox, who had been assembling his fascinating book on the Underground Church, told the 7,000 gathering that *Hair* was an appropriately Christian blend of "innocence and suffering."

Time reported that one well-dressed family munched their way through hamburger, malts and French fries during the Mass. The high selling magazine thought it was the splashiest rock Mass yet offered, but noted that *Hair* music had already made inroads into informal worship gatherings. And in American terms it wasn't exactly new to innovate with rock music. By this time *JCS* was making inroads and being seen by some as a Christian production. Interestingly it was this same week that saw the small off-Broadway theatre, Cherry Lane, give *Godspell* its first run.

It might well be asked as to where Jesus was in all this hullabaloo. Supporters would say that he hovered around and about in Spirit, that in its totality all this was about him and God.

Others, without belonging to any protest styled group, could say it was about people enjoying themselves and only occasionally touching the harsh reality of walking with a Christ to possible crucifixion.

Not unexpectedly, there were strident voices raised in anger. The Secretary, Conservative Evangelicals in Methodism, David G Sharp, wondered whether the Christian was now supposed to take on board that marijuana was a gift from God, that Christian love should now be extended to say that sexual promiscuity - homo – and hetero-sexual, are part of how Christian love shall be understood. Mr Sharp saw the whole thing as travesty of evangelism, of worship, of Christianity itself.

However *Hair* was not a piece readying itself for a forward looking Church assembly. It did not have to say anything Christian in an age of awareness.

The critics could shout, but they were doing so from the premise that any religious subject must needs first gain the imprimatur of official religious bodies. They were living in earlier decades and had not caught the new age dawning. The Church would have to create or be trampled upon.

Hair announced the dawning of the 'Age of Aquarius'. Some said soul searching had come to Britain. This was an age of increased awareness. Interest in Eastern religion and beliefs spread across popular culture. Those who stood back somewhat aghast did so from the basis that many of the groups offered a quick return of instant answers to deep questions. That did not stop thousands flocking to various organizations including The Inner Peace Movement which would claim 400,000 adherents worldwide. All this was grist to the mill for the people who launched *JCS*. It seemed almost natural that it should follow *Hair*.

Some who went to see *Hair* wondered what had happened to Jesus? Would anyone leave the show thinking they might follow him? Would you go away from the stage performance? This anger translated itself into a suspicion that theatre was anti-Christian, and it coincided with more ferocious assaults by Mary Whitehouse on the TV and radio output of the time. These two media forms were seen to be delivering ever-increasing volumes of bad language, violence and suggestive immoral behaviour. They were seen to be shaping society rather than reflecting it.

The other theatre production was *Son of Man* by Dennis Potter (1969). By the late 1960s the English writer had established himself as a lively and provocative playwright. He was associated with left wing politics and having graduated from New College, Oxford with a degree in philosophy, politics and economics, he worked as a journalist and critic. He wrote *The Singing Detective*, a six-part television drama, while in hospital suffering attacks of psoriatic arthropathy. Potter would die from cancer of pancreas with secondary cancers in the liver. In his final interview on television, with Melvyn Bragg, he talked of religion being the wound and not the bandage. He recalled very early life at Salem chapel in the Welsh coal mining area and singing from the 1,200 Sacred Songs and Solos "Will there be any stars in my crown when the evening sun goes down/When I wake up with the blessed in the mansion of the rest." He added, "And it makes me laugh, and yet it tugs me, and I see little kid's faces singing".

His works were not free from major criticism. *Only Make Believe* (1973) was considered indecent and *Brimstone and Treacle* (1975) was banned by the BBC for eleven years. *Son of Man* preceded these and in his depiction of Jesus as an earthly hippie he was accused of blasphemy.

The Jesus of Dennis Potter has a basic uncertainty about his own persona. At times he is seen as someone tormented by mental illness, at other moments he possesses the charisma of someone who can excite and control crowds. In other circumstances he is simply the Son of God. Long before Mel Gibson's *The Passion*, here was a Jesus subject to prolonged whipping, nailed to a cross and his crown of thorns drips blood. According to one reviewer, the staging by the Deep End Theatre Company at Cheltenham's Playhouse, saw the crucifixion harrowingly portrayed. Simon Lewis of BBC Radio Gloucester, wrote: "with hammers and nails echoing loudly, blood oozing down Jesus' battered body, and Martin Oakes' remarkably effective lighting, I gazed upon an image which will linger long after the audience has gone home." The Cheltenham production was directed by Sean Mayo to considerable acclaim.

Interestingly of course with *Superstar* in the offing here was a Jesus beset by internal doubt. There was also a somewhat villainous Judas, seen as a misguided devotee. Potter did major in an area that was partly mirrored in *Godspell*. This centres on the Jesus who explains what real freedom consists of. The most powerful passage on this is found in Act 11 scene six and pages 78-79.

Potter has Jesus saying that most people do not know what it means to be free. "You belong to God. You do not belong to Caesar. You belong to God." The question is posed – what does this mean? The answer is deceptively simple: "It means that you belong to yourself. It means that you belong to each other. You are all free." There is a secret that has been in existence since the world began. Jesus says: "Dare to listen and I will tell you how to change the world…..A light must be lit…the world need not always be in darkness…not always be filled with the hungry…There are better things that are yet to be seen. I will show you."

This section from the play is instanced in the book *Love and Meaning in Religious Education – The Incarnational Approach to Teaching Christianity*. It falls beneath a section title 'The Incarnation Basis of Eucharistic Celebration'. It follows text where the writers D.J. O'leary and Theresa Sallnow outline the situation where within the reality of Incarnation all experiences are 'redemptive; family life, friendship, work, study, leisure activities and every other dimension of our existence in the world.' At the same time this is shrouded in mystery, it is there to be found and realised, it does not come prescribed and portioned. It involves a wide spectrum of human experience. It suggests that "the pattern of true loving humanity established in Jesus, is the only paradigm for our actions and attitudes."

Obviously Potter puts his words into the mouth of Jesus, a dramatic technique which annoys some Christians, although I would suggest some of this criticism springs from misunderstanding.

The playwright has something in common with the preacher, in the sense that both are presented with the words of Jesus. Each digs behind the bald statements to discover their meaning. The preacher dissertates. The playwright does the same. Neither may get it right. Both can misinterpret. Essentially the aim rests in seeking what may have been the true intent of what Jesus meant. Obviously a writer can set out to distort and destroy for whatever reason, or deliberately, even playfully, construct provocative theories about biblical texts. Most would say this about Steven Berkoff's *Messiah* text, performed at the Assembly Rooms, Edinburgh, as part of the Festival in 2000. It was well described by Rachel Halliburton, in the London *Evening Standard* as portraying, "a colourful blood and guts portrayal of everything from the virgin birth to the crucifixion."

Off-stage, as it were, in unexpected quarters, there was a Jesus who cried "I am too late. I can't be crucified for men, because they've already crucified themselves." This Jesus appeared in Edward Bond's drama *Passion*. Bond's central thrust lay in utilising text to drive home the point that the West should dismantle its nuclear bombs. The play was featured at an open-air festival held by the Campaign for Nuclear Disarmament at a London race track in 1972.

In 1971, in the USA, Leonard Bernstein produced his *Mass: A Theatre Piece for Singers, Players and Dancers*. It was created for the opening of the John F. Kennedy Centre for performing arts in Washington D.C. It was an expression of Bernstein's fascination with the Roman Mass which he considered moving, mysterious, and eminently theatrical. The piece follows the liturgy precisely, but as Nina Bernstein says it is juxtaposed against frequent interruptions and commentaries by the celebrant and the congregation, much like a moving debate.

"There is stylistic juxtaposition as well, with the Latin text heard electronically through speakers or sung by the chorus, and the interruptions sung in various popular styles including blues and rock-and-roll. On the narrative level, the hour-and-a-half long piece relates the drama of a celebrant whose faith is simple at first, but gradually becomes unsustainable under the weight of human misery, corruption and the trappings of his own power."

The choir express their own doubts and suspicions about the necessity of God in their lives.

Eventually doubt gives way and it all ends with a hymn of praise, universal peace, and love. Jesus does not appear on stage and in fact his name is not mentioned. It has been subtly said that Jesus hangs invisibly around the wings like the Yahweh of Moses in the Bible.

The Mass drew heavy criticism from some quarters, and in later reflection Malachi Martin sees the Mass decked with sub-literate rubbish strung out with silences and reminiscent melodies.

"You see, the entire mystery of Jesus is no mystery. Let's be human about it, as we can be about sex, apple pie, the war, the flag, our country, personal honour, anything. For nothing is so untouchable that we cannot use it, in order to be human."

Martin sees both Bond and Bernstein simply picking up visible cues from the real world. He sees the two, and others could be added, who have set out to 'humanize' Jesus and everything connected with him. He instances a West Coast Mass service where the communion words become, "Take the body of Jesus, as you will shortly take the body of your girl." Indeed, this is realism Jesus, in other words "fashioned into whatever suits the behaviour, including the caprices, of any man and of any woman." Martin sees Bernstein using the figure of Jesus to represent the opposite of what Jesus achieved: salvation for all. "Even in man's modern disorderly theatre of longing and even for a Jesus figure, this is an impossible role. Exit Jesus. Exeunt all."

When *Jesus Christ Superstar* made its entrance there was for the innocent the hope that it would be a clean and healthy traditional portrayal of Jesus. For to those scratching around for something to make the Faith talked-about this could be what the nation needed. Church attendances would revive and most of young people would not let their eyes and minds be dulled by dark brown colours, endless pews, and dragging hymns. They would find a new happy family bustling with good things. They would be saved and book their passage to heaven. In the process, as one well-known British evangelist of the time believed, the young would cut their hair and find short back and sides the hair of a respectable believer, as would a tidy suit and clean shoes. Unfortunately the illustration is true.

Theatre had assumed in *Jesus Christ Superstar* a new significance. It was the first time in which a potential show was launched and sold to public and general media on the back of a record album. Without its success much else of similar nature would not have taken place. Eventually there would be the film, the video. It was initially thought to be a production for young people but while there was some interest in Britain it never touched the good vibes that came its way in the United States. As I shall suggest later there were particular circumstances that proved a welcome bonus for *Superstar*'s success.

It was the first musical to use rock to differentiate character. It also heralds a change in the nature of this book and how we co-authors have approached the subject of Jesus centre stage. The text and concept was an instant affair. It came from the immediate. It was a product of its time. The writers did not connect with classical tradition, or with history. It made the world of playwrights such as T.S. Eliot, Christopher Fry, John Masefield, Gabriel Marcel, Graham Greene, Charles Williams and Dorothy L. Sayers seem long distant. To reiterate a point made earlier, most of those named moved within the Catholic tradition as it survived in English churches. Lloyd-Webber and Tim Rice gave no notice that their concepts came out of such a world. Certainly, I know personally, that Tim loved pop music.

Going to the musical spawned discussion on the pyrotechnics rather than the story, or the characters. There would come an undue preoccupation with the visual Jesus, less with what he said, or meant in His own time and might mean now. This would affect even small religious based theatre companies who attempted through multi-media presentation to dramatise the Jesus story as they thought fit (usually claiming that they were true to Scripture and its revealed truth) and in Christian sources dare to correct the purported cardinal errors of *Jesus Christ Superstar*.

Here, in colourful and dramatic fashion the religious world almost lost its Jesus. *Superstar,* unlike the *Mysteries* had no intention to teach people the faith, let alone celebrate it for believers. It was not sponsored by church authorities (thankfully) or even the work of convinced card carrying Christians, although both writers, especially Lloyd-Webber could claim past religious association. It was simply that so many elements in the story of Jesus possess dramatic input. However, it was only an initial negative, for the churches were loved and cuddled rather than aggressively marched to the ticket office. The backlash and negative shouts came from some claiming to be Christians while their spiritual brothers and sisters were warming the seats of theatres worldwide.

This was an event underwritten by considerable money. It was part of show-biz, owned by it, exhibiting real glam. The kick-off was in some Wardour Street offices, a once famous London street full of agents and film studios. It was here that David Land had his office, where I spent considerable time when writing *Jesus In A Pop Culture*.

His brilliant management acumen combined with the various marketing associates won the day in persuading all who would hear that *Jesus Christ Superstar* would eventually conquer the world and become one of theatre lands most profitable works.

Land had been persuaded by seeing an earlier work *Joseph and the Amazing Technicolour Dreamcoat*, a pop cantata for children and which had been presented at *St. Paul's Cathedral*. He gave Andrew Lloyd-Webber and Tim Rice £25 a week to write the work and three years to complete it. They did it in less.

In a television programme Land said Jesus would be the next big thing in show-biz and the record industry. In 20th century terms this Jesus would be a superstar. However a superstar of the 20th century bears no mystery, it has to be instant. Superstars have a limited life for they belong in a saleable world where the new is discarded the moment it ceases to see a sales rise. Its arguable quality is irrelevant. The young are trained to look for the next best thing and in hip circles to jettison the same once it becomes public knowledge. It does not see, as the American theologian Paul Tillich wrote in his book *The New Being*, "power under weakness, the whole under the fragment, innocence under guilt, sanctity under sin, life under death" for only such a person can say: "Mine eyes have seen thy salvation."

These are not the themes of *JCS*. They are not concepts by and large that interest major theatre writers who have brought Jesus centre stage. That said, they are not always of interest to some Christians who much prefer to use religious jargon when it comes to Jesus, even if they do not actually understand what it is they are saying.

The business world has the luxury of seeing things simply as grosses, overheads and profits. That makes things all very straightforward, provided the shareholders receiver regular dividends.

The recording of *Jesus Christ Superstar* utilised the talents of well-known rock music names. Between October 1970 and December 1971 it sold three-and-a-half million copies. It was a double album that came in a special creative fold-out sleeve with 16 reproductions in full colour of paintings of Jesus. 12 of them by Old Masters and four of them by three boys and a girl from a school in south London.

The young people were asked to paint their pictures of Christ. The sleeve looks conventional enough but on the back it took an unusual unconventional twist in design. It opens in the middle of the back cover and four panels, pointed at each end, open outwards in each direction to form a star. At the time I wrote in the Church of Scotland magazine *Life + Work* that it vied with the *Beatles* and their *Sgt Pepper's Lonely Hearts Club Band* and *The Who's* epic *Tommy* as one of the bravest and most creative pieces to hit the rock audience. I did conclude the feature by saying, "*Superstar* is now a stage show in New York. It will arrive here in early summer. From reports, the show seems a far cry from the record. For the moment then, concentrate on the latter."

However it was the American market that largely bought the album and gave the single Superstar from Murray Head with the Trinidad Singers an eight week run in the top 40 whereas in Britain it made one entrance at 47 in the top 50 of the time. Here was the Jesus translated on to a 7" disc with the song asking what is the real Jesus. It was not likely to be found in such an arena.

A further British release from Yvonne Elliman of 'I Don't Know how To Love Him' reached the same position in Britain. Its overall success was hindered by radio station uncertainty whether they should play a record of a girl wondering how she could 'make it' with Jesus. In the States it reached number 26 and had a six week listing in Billboard's top 40. Apart from the media world giving innumerable mentions to *JCS* it set in motion an argument between people as to whether it should or should not be banned. It meant the American East Coast savoured first the stage show. It was launched at a Lutheran church in New York. The man from London's St Paul's Cathedral wrote some positive notes to say that everyone should buy the record, in this case the single,

Rice is recorded in Ian Bradley's absorbing book *You've Got To Have A Dream – The Message of the Musical* – as saying that key inspiration for the show's title song 'Superstar' (MCA MKS 5019), came from a line in a Dylan song "I can't think for you/ you have to decide/ Did Judas Iscariot have God on his side?"

When the album recording first appeared the BBC refused to play it. Rice thought this was because they either thought it was a "Billy Graham sort of thing or a straight-forward bit of blasphemy." Whatever the case it was wonderful free publicity!

In overall appeal, *JCS*, as it became in popular reference, achieved an astounding feat by crossing sacred demographic boundaries and so presented itself as the show for everyone. Hence extensive comment and consideration appeared in the young person's music weekly, the *New Musical Express* and at the same time in the *Church of England Newspaper*. Eventually there is a case for saying that the rock generation sniffed and left. Church people stayed and the original run and later revivals saw them arrive into London West End theatre land by the coach-load. In early times the clergy across the country were assiduously courted, especially by breakfast meets with the writers. In the 'religious' realm it had an ecumenical success story as some Protestants, Roman Catholics and Jews united in condemnation.

America gave this production one major uplift. It coincided with the still heady days of the Jesus Revolution, an enormous outbreak of religious faith amongst many young people and which had had its birth way back in the 1960s. In media terms the story broke via *Time Magazine* and its famous cover picture of a long-haired, bearded Jesus in the issue of June 21, 1971. It instanced the impressions of a Maureen Orth who said: "The first thing I realized was how different it was to go to high school today. Acid trips in the seventh grade. Sex in the eighth, the Vietnam War, a daily serial on the TV since you were nine and school worse than 'irrelevant' – meaningless. No wonder Jesus was making a comeback."

When *JCS* hit Broadway the streets swarmed with young people with their badges and banners and the insistent message: "Smile, Jesus Loves You." Queues stretched for several miles and it became the hottest thing in town. The young people, somewhat mistakenly, assumed this was the Jesus story for the converted, a time of praise and worship. For others, it was the Jesus they had been looking for, said and sung in a language they understood. They did not seem to realise they had lost Jesus who was called the Christ. To some extent they had gained Judas.

The talented and ambitious Lloyd-Webber and Rice saw Jesus as a fascinating man - the central character in a superb story. They took the last seven days in His life, put words and music to the story and eventually came a rock opera. It was two years in the writing and Lloyd-Webber speaks of many arguments on how it should be treated. Both saw themselves as not particularly religious and Rice to the chagrin of some dismissed the idea that Jesus is God.

What moved Tim Rice was the impact Jesus made upon people, one of colossal proportions. He told the *NME* writer Tony Stewart that it was a very narrow attitude that suggested you could not mix Jesus and rock 'n' roll. "If Jesus can't be discussed in today's terms then forget it, he can't be discussed at all." Some religious people would say that it depends on the character and style of the Jesus portrayed, others would posit the thought that Jesus was above the sometime crass machinations of popular culture, yet paradoxically the same voices would pray that Jesus would be known amongst the people.

Andrew Lloyd Webber apparently would have liked to have included the Resurrection but in the end to keep the peace they decided to go beyond the Cross to the garden and Jesus' tomb, but no further. It must have upset the first director of the New York production for it would have promised much visually. As it was, he says, it gave a final message of hope rather than despair. It left an open question as to whether Jesus did or did not rise from the dead.

However in a touring American production there seemed surety on one point, that Jesus could not be played by someone with short hair. Shawn Phillips was cast, a bearded Texan with silky hair down to his waist. It was noted that his hair was blonde in colour. Judas was given to a talented black actor Carl Anderson.

Whatever a writer may have in mind there is still the director and this person may give the impression of finding the writer's views inspiring and so deep, but in practice the director can adopt a cavalier approach and so weave his own little web. On Broadway, *Superstar* had Tom O'Horgan on board with another important person in set designer Robin Wagner. O'Horgan, who was diagnosed with Alzheimer's disease, died in 2009.

The two contrived some of the most spectacular effects seen on stage, although it might be said that some of the visual wonders stood tall on their own and disguised momentarily the fact that the show was a rock opera, let alone centred on Jesus. Whether O'Horgan was someone who saw a text to be visually rewritten by him is a subject for discussion. Certainly no one can deny he possessed a head packed with the unusual and stimulating, even if sometimes overblown and misplaced. Few can equal his 1971 run of shows on Broadway: *Hair, Superstar, Lenny* (a celebrative piece about another unusual human being, Lenny Bruce) and *Inner City*.

In O'Horgan's production Jesus' first appearance was stunning. This was not a modest carpenter's son from Nazareth but someone who was the belle of the ball. Jesus wore a shimmering white cloak, rising perpendicularly from an immense golden chalice. To the *Sunday Times* reviewer in 1972, it was if Jesus was squeezed from a tube of toothpaste. Extraordinary. Not surprisingly the major US magazine *Time* decided to run this splendid sight on its front cover on October 25, 1971.

There was much more to accentuate in some people the possibilities of a coronary heart attack. Extraordinary beyond extraordinary was the sparkling jock-strap worn by Judas. However super-super-extraordinary, and stretching the mind's continual push for sanity, was the ending. Christ is removed to Calvary and to quote Kane, "We are given an amazing storm as an entire stage cloth is inflated by a wind machine while distorted images are projected on to the resultant writhing balloon. Suddenly the storm dies away and an enormous eye that has been decorating the back-cloth during the entire evening opens to reveal Jesus Christ comfortably crucified on a huge golden triangle. It's as if the execution had been staged by *Heals*. The triangle slowly glides downstage until it hovers, seemingly without support, twelve feet above the orchestra grill. Truly, super, super, super, extraordinary.

It was for some watching a 'moment' never to be repeated, but always remembered with awe. Without intending to be irreverent or superficially clever, a watching Jesus in the heavens must have wished it might have been that way, albeit to clash with his decided mission once he emerged from the Temptations. Apart from that, it was truly a gay scene.

Australia followed the USA and a week after its opening in Sydney, show business empire superman Robert Stigwood brought over to Britain its director Jim Sharman. The 29 year-old said London will see something extremely beautiful and simple. It was hardly either of those two things. It was stark, it did possess pace, it did have guts and fire, and it was loud. He said he wanted the principal characters of Jesus, Judas and Mary to speak for themselves without any lavish gimmicks or costumes. Sadly British audiences would not be treated to any psychedelic crucifixion, huge angels with psychedelic wings shimmering, surreal sets, dancing dwarfs. Andrew Lloyd Webber and Tim Rice had found the Broadway Christ just a "little too vulgar." *The Guardian's* obituary notice on the American director quotes Andrew Lloyd-Webber as saying: "The floor of the stage was vertical, and as it went down, people swarmed over the top of it, "like ants."

Brian Thompson's design for the Australian production in 1972 has been described as minimalist but this should not be confused with a basically empty stage. His work set new standards for Australian musical theatre. Its centrepiece was an articulated, hydraulically-operated dodecahedron. Nothing of its size, complexity, and novelty had been seen on the Australian musical stage. During one Australian performance Jon English as Judas found himself the subject of presumed anger as he betrayed Jesus at the end of Act 1. A member of the audience threw $6 worth of 20 cent pieces raining down upon him and causing him to receive medical attention of some five stitches to the eye.

The British late summer 1972 version was indeed under-played compared with the Broadway work, even Herod had lost some of his campness.

As for Jesus, Paul Nicholas was not particularly well cast, Judas lacked necessary strength and to some extent the show lacked real gut wrenching thrust, but at least the good strength in writing and song came through much more noticeably. Stigwood whose track record before *JCS* displays a unique catholicity and a generous embrace of all things undressed with *Oh! Calcutta* and *The Dirtiest Show In Town* felt the show was immune from criticism. At the time he forecast a run of five or six years. As with his record business he knew a good thing when he saw it and *JCS* added to an impressive business portfolio.

Reviews were ten a penny, by and large they expressed praise, but other than the religious press there was little deep penetrative analysis on the Jesus we were seeing. The more liberal *The Christian Century* saw Jesus in a first-century setting with twentieth-century sensitivity. Derek Jewell of *The Sunday Times* thought it often more moving than *Messiah*. In the *Daily Mail*, Peter Lewis found it "a pageant-concert of simplified beat numbers." Naturally the academics had their say and decided the writers and their production seem to exist as a "post-modern Christological phenomenon." Jesus is being reduced and reinterpreted according to the values of a modern entertainment idol and no longer models the self emptying mandate, in theological terms, "to show us the Father."

JCS fetched considerable criticism from those who probably never saw it; sometimes it was of an unkindly nature from the Christian community, occasionally the general theatre reviewer. There were those who said the production did not preach Christ and was not a converting ordinance. Many walked the streets with banners proclaiming that Jesus was no superstar, he was the Son of God. *Christianity Today* from a basically conservative stance saw a Jesus who looks and acts incompetent, unsure of himself and petulant.

Some said their objection came from a distaste that the musical had not come through official church circles and therefore did not have the right approval. Whatever the case, thankfully it did not. It would have spent a year or two in the church sidings awaiting such approval, occasionally brought out for discussion by a committee. In some cases the motivation was simply to correct what some perceived as a misreading of the Gospel narratives.

Others felt its portrayal of Jesus sadly lacked finesse, and at worst it was blasphemous. The leading young person's Christian magazine of the time *Buzz* gave it their front cover and a double page spread inside the heading 'Jesus is no Superstar – He is the Son of God. Accept no Substitutes.'

In bringing together *Superstar*, and the other religious based musical of the early 1970s *Godspell*, the magazine said that "although they portray Jesus in totally different – and questionable – ways, the fact is Jesus is the 'hub' of these shows. No Jesus – no show." However, the writer, suggested a "Distinct gap between the Son of God and the son of money."

The most venomous religious voice came from one of church music's most revered commentators, Erik Routley. In the *Methodist Recorder*, March 2, 1972, he labelled *Superstar* "heretical and dangerous" and stressed that (good) doctrine matters. As he saw it, *JCS* presented a Christ who was good, but a failure, and "that the people who crucified him are to be hated for killing him. This is what I think the authors believe, wanted to say, and think right. The Scriptures tell me that this was a victory...." He thought *Superstar* encouraged all the wrong attitudes to the Atonement.

It was the American evangelist Billy Graham who complained that the musical asks who Christ is rather than affirming his divinity. Part of the famous lyric runs:

> Jesus Christ Jesus Christ
> Who are you? What have you sacrificed?
> Jesus Christ Superstar
> Do you think you're what they say you are?

Graham might have read further into the song for the suggestion is not simply one regarding divinity, but whether Jesus' thinking was developed or embroidered by what people told him. In other words he adapted according to those around him. That is to say he didn't really have a firm idea who he was or of his ministry. The Gospels, as I read them lend little support to such views. Jesus may have been mistaken, as indeed those sources that kept and told the stories surrounding him, but that is another matter.

In dramatic terms the former scenario of questioning is much more interesting and it leaves an audience to make its own journey, but a play in a secular setting is not Bible ministry, unless like the Hillsong community that meets Sunday by Sunday in London's Dominion Theatre it makes clear its position. Again, Graham illustrates, this facet of some Christians that assumes all forms of presentation shall serve their own interests. It has to realize that it has no privileges and must learn to fight in the battle for allegiance.

While Billy fretted, there was apparent joy from the Anglican Bishop of Liverpool, the Right Revd. David Sheppard. This popular evangelical simply told readers of his regular *Woman* magazine page (August 8, 1972) that, "I like this Jesus." He further told his audience, "Many young people today want to think of Jesus as their contemporary and I was very moved when I listen to this attempt to say within their pop culture what he means for some of them."

But was that the intent of the writers, that they were filling in as it were for a church that could not communicate?

The much admired Bishop found the brutality of the flogging and execution powerful. His agony real, but thought one important element was missing – that of victory. St John in particular saw Jesus in control all the way through and records his saying, "It is finished" and His meaning was, "It is accomplished, my work is complete." Sheppard also appreciated the moment when Pilate washes his hands of Jesus. Jesus has rejected the last offer, one that would have meant being spared of death by a cross. "At that moment, softly and with great dignity, the tune of *Jesus Christ Superstar* is played. He's that sort of Superstar who deliberately chooses to suffer for us."

Both Lloyd-Webber and Rice in interview often mentioned meticulous research; it appeared not to impress respected youthful Anglican clergyman, singer-songwriter Garth Hewitt. There was only the slightest give in his saying, "*Superstar* seems to treat these records (New Testament) as if they were not worth taking". He was scathing about how Jesus was portrayed. Other characters had lively and convincing personalities but as for Superstar? "Well, he didn't quite make it."

He thought no one would wish to follow the Jesus of *Superstar* let alone be someone you would die for. Judas seemed the most interesting, a "full-bloodied realistic character asking important questions." Erik Routley, in his review of *JCS* for *The Methodist Recorder*, reached a similar conclusion.

Hewitt writing in this further *Buzz* examination of the mega-success rock opera sees no sign of the Gospel narrative when Jesus is confronted by a crowd of poor and sick people and he screams at them, "heal yourselves". In the Garden of Gethsemane he admits, "I have changed, I'm not so sure as when we started, then I was inspired, now I'm sad and tired." This Jesus feels it is part of God's plan that he should die, but as to the point of it, He hasn't a clue. "This Jesus has no confidence, no idea whether he has a kingdom anywhere; he can only sigh, "If only I knew" and so the question is left open, "Jesus Christ, who are you?" Some of the issues raised by Hewitt found their way into the letters column of the *Methodist Recorder*, and one came from an undergraduate at Southampton University, whose views seem distinctly un-Hewitt.

The writer Martin J. King, a Methodist local preacher, thought there was a good contrast between Judas and Jesus. "Judas is portrayed as seeing Christ becoming aware of being someone special, unique and possibly more than human, and Judas is frightened by the possibilities this entails. Christ is portrayed as someone who is trying to discover himself, sometimes unsure of his role, as indeed was the Christ of Gospels." That is open to severe criticism.

In a smallish pamphlet John A. Coleman felt Tim Rice might be a fine writer and Andrew Lloyd-Webber a talented musician, and others skilled in the realm of theatrical production, but anyone so connected was out of his depth in presenting the subject of Jesus Christ. In fact they are utterly competent. The writer fears that if *Superstar* gains acceptance in religious circles, it will be followed by more religious rock and roll such as *Oh! Calcutta,* which was a "try out" for even more corrupt theatrical productions, so *Superstar* offered distortions of the Scripture record to make it fit for theatre use.

So what was it that grated when it came to presenting Jesus? Coleman says in the New Testament there is no glamour attached to the ministry of Jesus. He sees his message of repentance as unpopular, the basic following small – and that none of this equates with a Jesus of Hollywood or the rock world. This, said Coleman "was a blunder of the highest magnitude." The writer certainly increases his blood pressure for by page 18 he accuses the writers of a Satanic attack on the person of Jesus. He sees this man as the false Jesus. Whereas Billy Graham spoke of the production asking questions, Coleman says the musical is full of assertions. However, Coleman does agree with Webber on one point that it was only in recent time that such a work could have been presented: "Today, there is little that is held as being too sacred for this world of entertainment to touch with defiled fingers."

Ian Bradley would have us accept that *Superstar* was the first of the "gloomy, doomy, through-sung blockbusters that were to dominate musical theatre throughout the last three decades of the twentieth century." He sees the production both giving millions of theatre – and cinema goers – a highly original and theologically nuanced presentation of the life and death of Jesus, and leaving them with a host of significant questions about who he was and what he meant. "In raising these questions, it is in a way a much more theological work than Bach's great settings of the Passion narratives which are full of drama but accept the Gospel texts at face value."

In terms of the actor to play Jesus height was important, although there is no evidence in Scripture to suppose Jesus was over six feet tall, let alone that he might have been five feet. In terms of the visual for this work, and the costumes that could be designed, stature was important. Genuine long hair was more than useful, as of course was some kind of beard.

Such interesting comments do though raise other issues, and for one thing it assumes that Tim Rice's perceptions are true to the given text rather than twisting them to suit a pre-ordained scheme of things.

Whatever can or cannot be said there is always that wonderful 'human' element where two authoritative figures find total disagreement. *The Church Times* reviewer of the show's video is impressed that the image of Calvary at the end emphasizes Jesus' sacrifice. Johannine Bradley is not convinced that *JCS* conveys any sense of God's glory, either in the final moments or at any other point, and I would ally myself with him.

Costume has a considerable effect on the way the actor-Jesus walks, holds himself, and perceives the person (Jesus) at any given moment, and in relation to other actors and their roles. At times, in *Superstar* there is stage mayhem with the set changing in remarkable fashion, and so the actor playing Jesus must have the ability to co-ordinate with a heavy 'tech' set. This is not intended to cover all aspects demanded of the stage actor, merely the special demands in this instance made on the actor on Broadway, and his name is Jeff Fenholt.

By October 1971 there were some 30 *Superstar* productions all over the world. It was enough to give conservative evangelicals severe heartburn.

Whatever were the pros and cons of how it was perceived, and the quarter from which attention came, there is no doubt that within the Christian community it spawned many attempts to present the person of Jesus. Eventually when copyright embargoes became less irksome churches presented their own version. In early times considerable pressure was applied to ensure there were no other versions but the 'approved' one. When some Australian nuns were told they could not go adventuring with *Superstar* they were told that even God was subject to copyright.

Presentations continue, even in West Cornwall, among Methodists in the Mullion-Helston area, Easter 2009. Forty years previous such a presentation would have been seen by many as worshipping at the shrine of the Devil, and at very least misguided. Meantime the professional West End production has experienced revival.

Much of the background to the *Superstar* sales saga is located in the book *Jesus Christ Superstar – The Authorised Version (Pan 1972)*. Initially it is laid out in the form of the famous 1611 King James Bible. Some of the adverts that are reproduced could only for some have added to their distaste. Hence the wording:

> WE WISH TO INFORM YOU THAT MCA'S OFFICES WILL
> BE CLOSED ON DECEMBER 25TH IN OBSERVANCES
> OF SUPERSTAR'S BIRTHDAY.

At least they were sure when it was.

By the time of its late 1990s revival Lloyd-Webber had six productions currently playing. He was no stranger to criticism for just that, his musicals mocked as being good only for the average man, "for tired businessmen, blue-rinse matinee ladies and out-of-towners." Some said his success meant many productions failed to find a home.

It had its first major revival at the Lyceum Theatre, London, in 1996, touring in 1998, with Gale Edwards' production possessing considerable restraint. New York saw a modified version in 2000. The London designer John

Napier was one the stage world's finest, known for elegant staircases to full size helicopters.

The critics huffed and puffed, and audiences rose to their feet to acclaim this version. David Lister in the *Independent* said that after two decades, here it was again, a few hundred million pounds later. Some, including *The Daily Telegraph* writer Mark Steyn, remembered that the *The Observer's* drama critic Michael Coveney either by mistake or in a well rehearsed glorious ad-lib, had at a theatre conference referred to *Jesus Christ Superstar*. The London *Evening Standard* in a page feature by Jasper Rees on the designer captioned: "The man who brought JC down to Earth".

The London *Evening Standard* critic of some eminence, Nicholas de Jongh was right in saying the second coming was less camp, more campus, and yet even if hardly likely to create the furore that attended the original, it could still exert mass musical hypnosis. He found the revamped historic Lyceum gorgeous, the set less so. The atmosphere created was, "like a university campus in carnival mood."

He saw the stage filled with simple, clean-cut young apostles, who hoist the Son of God to stand on their shoulders as if he were some campus hero. What though of Jesus? Hard words here for the Jesus Jongh sees, as a temperamental petulant wimp, "at his happiest in the soothing lap of Joanna Ampil's sweetly sung Mary Magdalene."

At first Steve Balsamo's Jesus, "looks and behaves rather like a neurotic hippie, out of sorts in his first university year." The second act does move things on with a sharper momentum. Balsamo, "wilts and winces most movingly. And in the ironically despairing song Gethsemane he rises to a sustained falsetto of grief and foreboding."

The Tablet was represented by a Mr Tommy Burns, who had 26 years previous been inspired by the original. He was impressed. It had stood the test of time and achieved, "a much greater sense of universality than before." He was persuaded by some words of James Thane, the managing director of Webber's Really Useful Company, who had told him: "We've tried to make a show that is confrontational, that makes people think, but without all the show-biz hype."

Burns sees the confrontational aspect from the moment Judas breaks into the first song challenging some of the basic tenets of the Christian faith, including, "Jesus, you've started to believe that you've begun to matter more than the things you say." However, Burns is keen to comment, utilising a description given him by a colleague: "This is no irreverent rock star defying God and all that he stands for, still less, a 'warped Iago-like Jacobean malcontent.'" Burns says it was a jolt not Judas' rabid scepticism that lingered most in his mind, but, "the terrible sense of betrayal and falling away that he conveys on handing Jesus over at Gethsemane with a passionate kiss."

All was not well on the first night of November 19, 1996, for Tim Rice chose to go on a walking holiday in Lowestoft. His one-time partner expressed bitterness.

The rather splendid Theatre Royal, Nottingham, ran the show in 2004 with reviewer Steve Orme finding Judas a far more intriguing role than Jesus, "who is after all perfection personified." James Fox made his professional theatre debut as Judas. As for Glenn Carter, the reviewer found his playing of Jesus lacking the potency one might expect from the Son of God.

It was *Godspell* from John-Michael Tebelak with the musical score from Stephen Schwartz that gained most from the London and American triumph of *Superstar*, although in London terms it preceded *JCS*. It was the first overspill onto the London stage of a new genre that was proving profitable in America – shows either about God or Jesus.

Godspell bounced off Tebelak's view of Christ being, "a fun sort of guy." This in itself is enough to send blood pressures rising in many an evangelical, and for those of a more liberal nature the issue of whether Jesus told jokes and laughed is not in itself a frivolous matter. In 1993 Richard Buckner wrote his book *The Joy of Jesus* in which he attempted to say that Jesus used various types of humour in the Gospels, ranging from pure absurdity to subtle irony, from riddles to amusing parables. Buckner would have it that Jesus was the first to give us the smile of God.

This writer has studied for several theological degrees and read widely various New Testament commentaries, but the only commentary from a Christian, rather than Jewish source, that has seemingly spent any time on this theme is the much valued book *New Testament Ethics* by Lindsay Dewar. The writer majors at various points on how absurd some Jesus stories are unless it is realised that his Jewishness is sharp, crafted and possesses that wonderful sense of deprecating Jewish humour. The stories come alive. Unfortunately many a Christian remains painfully ignorant of the Jewishness of Jesus. In May 2005 a former Methodist Vice-President, John Aldridge, in the guest sermon section asked the question 'Did Jesus Laugh?'

He pointed out that the great masters have painted thousands of pictures of Jesus in majesty, in agony, in prayer, but Jesus laughing? And there is a website which provides portraits of a heartily laughing Jesus (www.jesuslaughing.com).

Tebelak's words to the press in 1974 were not said in any crafted manner. Nor were they spoken with a public relations or press officer hovering in the background. In suggesting Jesus was a 'fun sort of guy' there came thoughts to me that he would in a modern sense wear sandals, chinos, a Ralph Lauren T-shirt from the local charity shop, and be known as a good raconteur, carrying around his iPod with favourite downloads, and looking for the nearest synagogue. Yet that somehow becomes an American Jesus, and to think that way is synonymous with the persuasive pull of American thought on Christian matters.

In more useful terms Tabalak saw Jesus as someone who realized that the solemnity of much church ritual and order blotted out the simple message that religion is essentially love and joy. The writer said he intended his writing as an indictment against the Church for keeping religion so serious and removed from the people. Whereas I have my modern conception of this good guy, the Jesus of *Godspell* is a clown with a red bubbly nose, painted eyes and fuzzy hair. It was, as John Harrison of the *The Daily Express* said in 1974, a "formula of fun without insult."

Tabalak's Jesus is one who assumes the goodness and all-pervading will of God and this enables him to feel complete freedom in living. This Jesus has unlimited compassion tempered with ability to read a situation and people in general. One reviewer, David Goodbourn, saw Jesus played like some, "naked Freudian ego – totally unprotected and so open to every hurt which comes its way. But open to every person as well."

The production carefully regulated pace. The impending sense of a Cross evident in the Gospels in the early days is restrained and eventually only there by simple use of a face slap at one point by Jesus to Judas. Suddenly the Supper is upon us. At the end Jesus is held high on the backs of the broken followers. He is not dead for the reprise says 'Long live God.'

This writer attended a preview at the Roundhouse, Chalk Farm, London, and met the cast. One of them, Jacquie-Ann Carr told me that it could be something fantastic, and of course as with *Superstar,* it has now been played throughout the world and continues to be performed. Its stage set and overall casting and crew can be a good deal less demanding than *JCS*. However when true to the spirit of Tabalak it is far from a simple proposition to cast Jesus.

The text is of course by far not the only important element in any musical: for one, there is the music, and in this case a number of catchy songs. There is the casting. For some, including this writer, David Essex as Jesus was inspirational casting for the first London run. He was comparatively an untried actor and successful pop singer, with a delightful ease about him, a marvellous smile, and a vivacity and aliveness. He could not portray a wooden Jesus if he tried.

Further praise came his way after the opening of the film version on May 31, 1973, at London's Odeon Haymarket and St Martin's Lane where many reviewers found Victor Garber's playing of Jesus fairly weak against the Essex stage performance. Micheal Jacob, one of the most perceptive writers in the religious field of the time found Garber's "gentleness not far removed from weakness and where he should dominate he seems merely petulant." The film scored most for its brilliant visual choices.

Unlike the spectacle of *Jesus Christ Superstar*. In whatever area is chosen, from costume to set, *Godspell* gave you a cast of young actors dressed in old jeans that became replaced by gaudy silks and satins and if at one time the text carried the words of people like Sartre and Thomas Aquinas it moved into the sphere of the wild and rugged John the Baptist. The cast exuded what drama directors and teachers call 'centred' and so for instance an air of naturalness with no false layers loaded on to the text, something that seems effortless and just comes. David Goodbourn's correlation of *Godspell* with *Hair* comes in noticing a cast nearly always on stage at the same time, alternating dancing with dialogue starting with laughs and going on to tragedy, and a mixture of music. That said, it is a pretty much used way of presenting a piece.

Essex was not a church-going East End lad and his most likely worship centre would be Upton Park and the club with whom he might have made a career as a football player; West Ham United. In terms of Jesus, he said, "At first I thought the idea of me playing Christ rather strange. I had this concept of Christ as man who wore white robes and performed miracles and didn't understand how a person like myself could play it. But when the producer unfolded the idea of the show I knew it was a part I could do."

When asked what he had got from the show Essex said he realized that Christ wasn't as heavy as he was made out to be. A similar statement was made by Murray Head in terms of his involvement with *JCS*. In my interview at the time with the actor who played Judas, Head said Jesus was one of the better, perhaps one of the few really good human beings to live on this often war-ridden planet. His own philosophy veered toward karma.

He told me: "There's a Judas in us all. I often think of the betrayal. I think I would align myself to some kind of naivety of a Geldof but I haven't got his way to do the kind of things he's done with Live Aid. I hope good does win, though like I said, the figure of Judas stalks."

Essex says: "It's a very weird piece of theatre; it plays on so many different levels. Clergy who know everything we say backwards come along and love it; yet also some dumb-head can come along and enjoy it equally for the music and the dancing." As for Jesus, the clown, Essex remarked: "Probably first of all because the clown is always the victim but never quite defeated, then there's the idea off behind the clown's make-up there's a lot of pathos."

He could have instanced Samuel Howard Miller who said, "Even the simplest clown manages by gesture and incident to explore the mythology of self. He too, like the saint, extends the dimension of consciousness beyond its normal limits. His ritual has its own sanctity as it elicits from us all the subtler dramas of our destiny."

Michael Watts in the music paper *Melody Maker* saw it as a great advert for God and thought that even, "the fiercest atheist could not fail to be moved by its mixture of broad humour, intense pathos and inherent simplicity of spirit." Watts said the message might be described as "dig thy neighbour." His final brief paragraph noted that it did not have the razzamatazz of *Superstar* or *Hair* but as he put it, "if it fails to do equally as well there is no justice on Heaven and earth."

Buzz on *Godspell* said it was "not a 'Christian' show in the sense that many would mean it. It does not set out to be so. But its contents are orthodox, positive and biblical. And that must be good." That didn't stop the boring Christian extremists and intolerants from coming out of their hide-aways and radiating distaste that Jesus should be seen as a clown. Obviously they assumed 'clown' was a figure of fun. That can be forgiven, but what is not acceptable was the crusade of hate that came his way.

We met sometime after his run and at the time he had gone into the West End production, *Mutiny*, at the Piccadilly Theatre. David said he still remembered with sadness and hurt the invective to which he was subjected by some Christians. "I was, after all, just an actor who had got this part, not some crusading evangelist. I got all this literature accusing me of this and that, terrible stuff, really was sickening. Loads of the stuff arrived daily. It turned me off all this church stuff – I thought if that was what it was all about or those were the people, stuff it." Yet the longer he played the part the more impressed he became by the teaching of Jesus and thought "it would be marvellous if we could live our lives as his teaching suggests."

Godspell has been much performed by church, amateur and drama school groups. As with *Superstar* it has had a major British theatre revival. In the autumn of 2007 it resurfaced with more than a hint of 'fill the seats' syndrome in the casting of Stephen Gatley, the former star of hit pop outfit *Boyzone*. Whether his teen girl following enjoyed seeing him crucified, albeit in a cheap looking and drab polyester jacket and jeans, is not documented. Gatley brought to Jesus his cherubic features, a pleasant voice and a touching niceness. Alfred Hickling in the *Guardian* runs *Jesus Christ Superstar* and *Godspell* into one thought when he says, "almost forty years later, they tend to blur into a single haze image of flower-child apostles performing parables in dungarees."

Both *Superstar* and *Godspell* achieved limited success in a film context. The overall distance between the two translated on to this form, for *Superstar* was very much De Mille with a touch of Ken Russell, and everything almost 'over the top', whereas *Godspell* kept its folkie image, and the costumes might have been purchased at a local flea market on the day of filming.

JCS the film was shot in Israel with a fourteen week schedule, and cast of 46 that included some extras. *Godspell* set up camp in New York with a cast of ten, the same as the stage production. It is said that the cost of *JCS* the film was $4.000.000, while *Godspell* was a quarter of that figure.

Both clung to their stage concept of Jesus, the differences lay more in the visual, and in *Godspell* you see John the Baptist pushing a cart through Garment District. People are baptized in Central Park. One scene is shot on top of then new World Trade Centre on the southern tip of Manhattan Island; use is made of the garden at the united nations, a pier on the river and the Statue of Liberty. It would seem most if not all of New York received a cast visit! Perhaps here Jesus did become a claimant of American citizenship

The music productions attracted criticism from a general misunderstanding of the nature of drama. Unless it is stated a writer is not offering a quasi-documentary, it is quite clear if it is simply, (as is the case for several) an actor reading a Gospel from the King James. However even there the text is being translated in speech patterns and overall understanding. It will be affected by the demeanour and stature of the actor, from vocal tone to physicality. The words can find a different meaning from the use of space.

The writer chases after new insights or is looking for a new way of revitalising what has become jaded in its appeal. In both these instances their writers were not concerned with presenting material that might gain the approval of the religious community. There was no known market, although admittedly once established that there was the chance of success it was sound marketing to persuade the religious community to put their bums on seats. Christians did not have to come but they did.

It can hardly be denied that Christians, let alone anyone else, have the right to object to how their story is told on the stage, but a stage presentation is not a worship or revival or a converting process. It is not there to tell a whole story, as indeed *Superstar* takes those last days of Jesus, or as with *Godspell* focus on the teaching of Jesus and His underlying attitude. It is also a strange mantra of some Christians that the Gospels tell all and that they should be left alone. Manifestly they do not. We have to surmise how individuals felt and reacted, what they thought, how moments altered perceptions, the shouts and cries of particular moments, the reasons for statements and actions. The scholar will aid us in seeing why the stories occur, where they find place, why there may be differences in emphasis or detail. They may point to why a particular Greek work is used.

Much more can be said, but it is abject nonsense to assume that the Gospels tell all. In any case their object is to illustrate particular beliefs about Jesus. They are not psychological studies. Material is not chosen at random. As such they are interested in one person Jesus and all else finds its centre in his existence.

CHAPTER FIVE

Plays, Plays And Plays

Play list in order of appearance
(across then down, numbers refer to subheadings)

Jerry Springer – The Opera	1	Corpus Christi	1
Queen of Heaven	1	The Mysteries	1
Messiah (Berkoff)	2	Paul	2
Last Days of Judas	2	Jesus my Boy	2
Whistle Down the Wind	2	Dating Jesus	2
Little Baby Jesus	2	Black Jesus	2
Jesus was a City fan	2	Not the Messiah	2
New Testament	2	Witness	2
The Guantanamo Years	3	On the Third Day	3
Jesus Hates Me	3	Tommy	3
See Me Hear Me	3	Jesus Hopped the A-Train	3
Jesus: The Wasted Years.	3	The Passion (US text)	3
Cotton Patch Gospel	4	In Arabia We'd All Be Kings	4
Canadian Badlands Passion Play.	4	Wolverhampton Mystery Cycle.	4
Jesus and Mohammed	5	Liberating Jesus	5
The Black Album	5	Simply Heavenly	6

Mama I Want to Sing	6	The Amen Corner	6
The Pitmen Painters	6	Doubt – A Parable	6
Blues for Mister Charlie	6	Jesus Moonwalks the Mississippi.	6
Gospel at Colonus	6	Candles in the Window	7
The Legacy of Dietrich Bonhoeffer	7	Giotto a Non Giotto	7
Song of Bernadette	7	St. Catherine of Siena	7
The Cost of Freedom	7	The Mountaintop	7
Luther	7	Gethsemane	8
Racing Demons	8	Angels in America	8
Love the Siner	8	His Dark Materials	8
Rent	8	The Last Confession	8
Rent Boy Ave – A fairy Tale		A Matter of Life and Death	8
The Screwtape Letters	8	Blasted	8
Harry's Christmas	8	Major Barbara	8

As compared to my extensive treatment of such plays and musicals as *The Man Born to be King*, *Jesus Christ Superstar* and *Godspell*, I am concerned in this chapter to look in less depth at a considerable number of plays about Jesus premiered at general theatre level. For a variety of reasons virtually all these texts do not lend themselves for presentation by church drama groups. On occasions they have provoked outright protest from mostly fundamentalist wings of the Christian family.

There is a view held by some Christians that Jesus is very much neglected and ignored once you step beyond their parameters. They believe there is a bias in the media against them. The facts do not support this. The performing theatre schedules feature Jesus far more than any other person, although the Jesus of playwrights may not always mirror the Jesus in orthodox Christian circles. The question Christians should be asking is why so many plays about Jesus and religion in general come from supposed non-believers?

Conversely that leads to the other question: why do so few quality plays come from the pens of known Christian or religious based writers?

Almost invariably the plays I have seen traverse a number of themes. It would be a simpler task if plays about Jesus fell into a straight-forward listing and were New Testament centred. Thus we could have plays that illustrate the parables of Jesus, or the miracle stories, or simply his teaching, events in his life; his crucifixion. On a church level plays of this kind can be found. There are many collections of short sketches and occasionally you can find a drama of an hour or more duration. Often there is no story line of consequence, no plot, no character development. In many a so-called biblical play the characters are merely puppets to repeat the lines found in Scripture.

However, obstacles or not, in an effort to prevent this chapter becoming a mere listing, I have categorized plays under subject headings, always conscious that there are elements in the chosen text which make this strict division somewhat misleading.

1. Plays concerned with the gender and sexual disposition of Jesus.

This is a rich area of text, albeit controversial. The recent most popular play that touches upon this theme is surely *Jerry Springer – the Opera*. It had a British national tour and ran at London's Cambridge Theatre in 2005.

The stage presentation mirrored the television plot, so we have the public confessional where individuals discuss their bad ways and meet with those who had figured in their mishaps. Obscure sexual predilections are mixed with mind-blowing stories of human betrayal. The show's carefully contrived plot includes a baying audience who appear to care little that fellow humans were being stripped of their dignity. Its concept and execution has been condemned by some, but for others it was compulsive viewing.

The second act particularly illustrates why this play falls beneath the general description of sex and gender. Here we see the devil forcing compere Jerry Springer to stage a version of the show in hell. The devils asks him to reconcile good and evil, God and the devil. As the reviewer Alan Bird wrote: "The devil demands an apology from God. Jesus is revealed as a 'little bit gay' and gleefully threatens condemnation on all those who 'piss him off'". Mary accuses the Christ child of parental neglect and God the Father sings 'it ain't easy being me'. By way of contrast Arthur Matthews, co-writer of the long running TV series, *Father Ted*, thought it "brilliant". A local vicar wrote to the Plymouth *Evening Herald* saying that the second half of the show made him feel like he was "in hell".

In the play *Corpus Christi* by Terrence McNally premiered at the Manhattan Theatre Club, New York City, the Christ figure is used to tell an all too frequent modern story of homophobia with attendant division, hatred, and hypocrisy. Jesus is shown as a rebel, a homosexual. Some might recoil at the words of Alex Eades in describing the 2005 Edinburgh Fringe Festival production discussing the possibility of Jesus being a homosexual: "He may or may not have been. Does it really matter? Does it contribute to the heart and soul of the story? What the company do with it means the play just comes across as being pointless and boring." If you are homosexual you might wish such a statement to be made, one that affirms your own identity.

The story line did follow the New Testament script, with some differences. Joshua, a young man, is the Jesus who from an early age experiences a non-accepting environment. He flees from his home in search of a welcoming community. He finds some like-minded and suffering people and so brings together a group of disciples who find his words of love and tolerance acceptable. Eventually he returns to the place of his upbringing, but he is betrayed by his lover Judas, and so crucified in front of the people who originally caused him to leave.

His final plea is that we should see all people as being equal in the sight of God. It falls on deaf ears. On the last page of script the actor playing John says the end is still to come, that what has been seen and heard represent the first birth pangs of a new age. During the play the writer calls upon Gospel stories and events, whether it be the Feeding of the Five Thousand, the event of Lazarus, or the Sermon on the Mount.

The Tron Theatre, Glasgow November 2009 was the venue for *Queen of Heaven*, part of the annual city Glasgay! Arts Festival, where Jo Clifford, a transsexual acted out her one woman play. The central thrust of the play revolves around the return of Christ, but this time as a female transsexual.

Jo, once John, told *The Independent* newspaper that, "I think it is very sad that the protest has enlisted Christians who have difficulties with gays and transsexuals. I wanted to point out that this does not have any foundation in the Bible. The people who angered Jesus were the scribes, Pharisees and hypocrites – the people who were deeply prejudiced were those who passed judgement on people they did not know.

At least the *Church Times* thought its readers should be in the know and sympathetically interviewed the writer-actor and explored the play's content. Jo told Tom Baldwin of the *Church Times*, "My original intention was to have Mary Magdalene as a transsexual prostitute. But when I sat down to write to my astonishment it was Jesus. So I thought: 'Alright, that's what I'd better do'". Previous to this she had written *God's New Frock; Jesus, Queen of Heaven* was its sequel.

Glasgow's Roman Catholic Archbishop, Mario Conti said it was, "difficult to imagine a more provocative and offensive abuse of Christian beliefs." The Pastor of Zion Baptist Church, Jack Bell said that "if the prophet Mohammed had been treated in this way there would have been a strong reaction from the Islamic community, but that just wouldn't happen." The organisers had hoped that the production would move to a larger seating capacity than the mere 25 at the Tron, however a 32 per cent rise in homophobic attacks in the city was noted.

Various comments appeared on internet sites. One said, "A transgender Jesus. A great idea. One of the problems with Christianity is that it is a masculinist creed, therefore how can it have any universal significance?" So what changes if Jesus is or became a woman? Or does He have to be both sexes at the same time? It becomes ridiculous. Another writer reminded people that throughout the history of Christianity, people have portrayed Jesus in their own image, both physically and philosophically. People have portrayed him as white and blond, dark and semitic, black and Asian. His words have been quoted to justify war makers and peacemakers. However the writer concluded that as Jesus was a "Jew, and given the condemnation to homosexuals in Leviticus it is highly unlikely that Jesus would have approved of same sex relationships. But why wouldn't a Jesus returned to earth have political and social attitudes in keeping with the times?"

Naturally some hard edged comments, "This creature is an abomination" came from the presumed religious community. In another case, "transsexuals or transgender are a group of people who seek protected status to pursue their fetish lifestyles of autogynephelia." There was comment to the effect that "I'm not a Christian, but it strikes me funny that these 'brave artists who mock Jesus' are not quite brave enough to mock Mohammed." Among some gay people who appreciated the text there was the feeling that critics had no respect or sympathy for those who wished to resolve their religion and sexuality/gender identity.

A much more eloquent gender apportioning, for which there is theological evidence in Scripture came by way of the brilliant 33-strong, all-black Isango Portobello Theatre Company who appeared at the Garrick, London, Autumn 2009, with *The Mysteries*. Here was a religious production with no white faces and God and Jesus black and female. Not withstanding a greater tolerance level in Britain, this was a brave statement from a group based in a country as patriarchal as South Africa. Pauline Malefane told the *Saturday Times Review*, that she simply can't be bothered with those who carp and criticise.

Each of these texts provoked hostility, not least in the crowds that gathered outside theatres in Plymouth on the *Jerry Springer – The Opera* tour. Hundreds gathered in an effort to stop the show. Supporters of a self-appointed organization Christian Voice prayed outside for the souls of the cast. The *Independent on Sunday* named the group's leader Stephen Green as being the individual causing *Jerry Springer* the most grief. The theatre world was dismayed by these developments and in May 2005 at a meeting organised by theatre managers there was concern expressed at what was seen as a growing intolerance in Britain, although it was felt that a tiny minority were "punching above their weight."

There were reminders of the protests against performances of *Jesus Christ Superstar* and more recently violent protests at Birmingham Repertory Theatre over the production of *Bezhti*. Some 400 people had thrown bricks through windows. The director of the Birmingham Rep, Jonathan Church said he had made the fatal mistake of talking to the Sikh community in a manner that suggested the theatre was willing to discuss the play's content and perhaps make changes. It was felt that the protesting religious groups had no idea of theatre, no understanding of the concept of fiction and who felt religious beliefs were not the province of the playwright unless the said person was wholly sympathetic to the faith being dramatized.

Disquiet was also expressed at the growing interference from political sources; in particular local authorities who had a financial stake in local theatre and were increasingly less concerned with free speech and more with appeasing voters.

It was the moral Right who protested in Manhattan at McNally's, *Corpus Christi*, as was also the case when the play came to Edinburgh. 300 protesters gathered at the Tron parading outside with candles, singing hymns and holding placards refuting the very idea of Ms Clifford that Jesus might in His second coming be a female transsexual, by proclaiming "Jesus King of kings, Not Queen of Heaven," and God: "My Son is not a Pervert." Anything is possible.

2. *Here I choose some play texts that directly or indirectly focus on the person of Jesus.*

Steven Berkoff's stirring 'in yer face' *Messiah* had an airing at Edinburgh's Assembly Rooms during the Festival, August 2000. It achieved major newspaper coverage and not least because one night Jesus went missing. *Messiah* has one of those great but rare openings that can surely only come on a wing and a prayer. This one wins. The stage is bare. There is silence. Jesus stands. Crucifixion looks imminent. The disciples are behind him, a rigid row of blank faces. One actor becomes a human sculpture. Jesus walks down the line and moulds each body. As Rachel Halliburton said in the *London Evening Standard*, "the cast is positioned like a frieze in a medieval church." Described in some quarters as irreverent, subversive and distasteful, this is a Jesus play where "sex and pissing and laddish jokes abound." It makes *Superstar* look more like the end piece of a well-ordered scouts' weekend. His Jesus is interested in fostering some kind of revolution. His Jesus "fantasises about dying on the cross and cynically manipulates the Scriptures."

The accomplished and prolific playwright Howard Brenton's play *Paul* was performed in 2005 at London's Cottesloe. Brenton, following a definable trend in writers portrays Jesus as rather drab and uncharismatic. *The Methodist Recorder's* reviewer, its Editor-in-Chief Moira Sleight, saw nothing in the play deserving of Christian protest, however she was hardly enamoured of Jesus played by Pearce Quigley. She sees a confused, enigmatic figure. That sits at odds with the fact that Paul was inspired by a Messianic figure. There was something so demanding about this fellow Jew that made him leave the comfortable situation of being a respected figure within Jewish mainstream circles. In the play there is no resurrection for Jesus, for he dies secretly in Syria.

On this occasion the publicity outfit did not wait for expected criticism. Its promotional blurb called it "an irreverent, provocative play." Some 200 or more letters were received before it opened. In theatre terms it was absorbing. Brenton was apparently an atheist son of the vicarage.

London's Almeida presented Stephen Adly Guirgis' *The Last Days of Judas*. This play portrays Jesus through the eyes of Judas. This text saw the writer favouring his love for scenarios dealing with law and justice that can have arguments flying here, there and everywhere, The big question posed by the play was whether Judas deserved hell for his deeds, be they intentional, misguided or deriving from his misunderstanding. There was tongue-in-cheek sign in the gallery of a set with just two desks and a slate and pebble floor that said with delightful nonchalance 'In God We Trust.' In the production the Devil wears Gucci, Simon the Zealot is a hoodie with an iPod, Judas enjoys his cigarettes and playing games with his basketball.

Jesus My Boy by John Dowie played at London's Pleasance Theatre and the writer placed Jesus in the context of his fathers' memory. In Scripture the story of Joseph comes in a handful of verses and so Dowie had to fill in the lines for Joseph. For him Joseph was a forgotten man and displaced father. At the same time he set the story of Jesus in its political context. The celebrated British actor Tom Conti played Joseph.

Obviously not intended to be a follow-up to *JCS*, Jesus returned to the London stage, at the Aldwych, courtesy once more of Andrew Lloyd Webber in his 1998 production of *Whistle Down The Wind,* the main character, a criminal played by Martin Lovett. Robert Butler of *The Independent* said that, "Webber has kept the title and thrown out the movie." In the film the actress Hayley Mills discovers a murderer who takes refuge in a barn, and believes he is Jesus.

Like *Les Miserables,* the libretto of *Whistle Down The Wind* makes substantial use of religious imagery and references. Jesus receives 24 mentions, the Saviour seven. Ian Bradley, in his excellent book *You've Got to Dream* saw the criminal enacting a figure not "unlike the angst-ridden Jesus of *Superstar* wrestling with the question of his identity and with such deep subjects as the nature and value of prayer." In the song 'Unsettled Scores' Bradley finds a common empathy with the *Superstar* song 'Gethsemane' again raising questions as to the identity of Jesus.

Dating Jesus focused on a single mother sex-obsessed poet who searched for salvation while losing her mind.

Little Baby Jesus was presented at London's fringe Oval House as of a trilogy of texts; it centres on the lives of three inner London school children.

Black Jesus by Oladipo Agboluaje is the story of mental case Omo becoming the Messiah in Brixton, London.

Traditional Christians, and especially those of Right Wing leanings, could hardly appreciate *Jesus is a City Fan,* which being interpreted implies that Jesus would have followed the Manchester football team which wears blue shirts, rather than the red of Manchester United. In the somewhat extraordinary text, the worldwide press are trying to find "the child born after being cloned from one of three DNA samples of the Turin shroud." The new Jesus turns out to be a 27year-old Manchester City supporting Luke. In the play City beat United by four goals to one.

Creating something of a minor storm there was Eric Idle's amusing *Life of Brian* and its adaptation as a musical *Not the Messiah*. A full length version was performed at London's Royal Albert Hall, 2009 to commemorate the 40th anniversary of the original *Monty Python* television programme. BBC Radio 3 also broadcast a recording of this performance on New Year's Day 2010 with the BBC Symphony Orchestra and Chorus. In true farce style, in the text Brian is mistaken for the Christ although clearly not him. Idle's work was not appreciated by some Christians. In a somewhat alarming occurrence, *Not The Messiah* was removed from the broadcasting schedules of the popular Classic FM station after people calling themselves listeners who were Christians made complaints. It was naturally a gift to the ever watchful British Humanist Association, described in one Google entry as the "national charity representing the interests of the large and growing population of ethically concerned, non-religious people living in the UK."

New Testament is an American play by Neil La Bute. In the play that is about a play, the main character, Jesus, is cast as Chinese. His ethnic background causes dismay, there is a move to replace him. He is defended on the premise that if Jesus is Love, couldn't anyone of any nationality be so cast?

Witness was premiered in November 2010 at the Michaelhouse, Cambridge. The play from the Cameo Theatre Company is based on the highly commended set of five plays of the same name originally broadcast on Radio Four, December 2007. The text is based on the Gospel of Luke. The radio series won the Stanford St Martin award for radio drama in 2008. The writer was Nick Warburton who apart from writing regularly for the TV series, *Holby City*, has written one or two short plays on religious themes.

3. *There are a number of plays that place Jesus or*
   Christian faith in a contemporary context.

The Guantanamo Years is a 60 minute monologue, which played The Black Box, Belfast, later in June, 2007, London's Arts Theatre. The writer postulates the scenario of God returning to earth in Jesus with the intention of explaining the intrinsic truth of Christianity. Jesus appears wearing a somewhat garish jumpsuit for a projected tour (God is seen as too old to start travelling at His age) which runs into problems. There is the detail that he was born in Palestine and it is recorded that he is an Israeli radical troublemaker. So what happens to him? The answer rests in the title, for indeed he is shipped off to Guantanamo. He is arguably the only Jew in the ill-fated camp. However, at least for a while, Jesus disappears from view, since the writer wishes to launch an attack on the West's war on terror and the nature of Guantanamo. Jesus reappears. He condemns the prison and its methods as unchristian. He escapes from the prison and wishes to find a place that accords religiously with his views, where they know how to deal with terrorists. This leads him to Belfast via the Gulf Stream. Belfast is not the answer so he moves to Dublin. He has been persuaded by the UDA.

Few reviews can have been more damning than that written by one of theatre's most famous critics Nicholas De Jongh of *On The Third Day*. It was staged at London's New Ambassadors Theatre, June 2006. The play by Kaye Betts had won a national competition for new playwrights. Jongh found much of the text absurd, and indeed suggested that "practising masochists interested in experiencing the oppressive boredom and angry bewilderment that a chronically inept piece of theatre can induce, should rush to savour" the piece. Thirty year-old Claire wishes to lose her virginity and invites Jesus back to her flat and pleads that he might snuggle beneath the bedclothes. Wisely Jesus does not go along with her plans; he goes potholing and even hosts a dinner party.

Jesus Hates Me by Wayne Lemon was set in a small Texas town where the miniature golf course bears the name 'Blood of the Lamb', with mannequins from *Wal-Mart* dressed to look like Bible characters. One mannequin gazes down from a wooden cross near the 17th hole. The text explores the life of people who over time have become shadows of themselves with only the menu of booze, drugs and sex to make life bearable. Along the way we meet Annie for whom the Lord's presence is her salvation. In the character of Annie's Ethan, aged 25, we have someone who challenges the ability of Christ's power to heal while at the same time hoping it might be true. Ethan believes, "God is playing whack-a-mole with us" and that Jesus sacrificed himself for us "just so we can screw around and not burn for it." As writer Eric Marchese observes, despite his cynicism, Ethan, "can't help but ponder what Christ's salvation must feel like. Did Christ have any regrets? he asks, and 'what else went through his mind?"

Pete Townshend of rock group *The Who* devised the rock opera *Tommy*. Initially released as a record, later as a film. *Tommy* the musical opened at La Jolia Playhouse, San Diego, California, June 1992. The Broadway debut was at the St. James Theatre, June 22 1993. It ran for 899 performances and 27 previews, finally closing June 17 1995. The original cast record, as opposed to the record release, came in July 1993. In 1995 a Canadian production opened in Toronto. Eventually it reached London's Shaftsbury Theatre and ran for just under a year with Paul Keating playing Tommy and pop star Kim Wilde playing Mrs Walker.

It did attract the religious press, including the bi-monthly *Crusade*, and where the reviewer Peter Cousins given generous space in the May issue followed one of the religious heroes of the time, H.R. Rookmaker in noting the cry of Tommy: "I crave the taste of reality." Another cry from Tommy is "See me, feel me, touch me, heal me!" but Tommy is deaf, dumb and blind and totally unrelated to anything or anybody. Visiting guests ask how he can be saved since he can neither hear nor talk about Jesus. In an amazing flash-back to the time when his senses deserted him he is able to see, hear and talk and good fortune leads him into becoming something of a Messiah figure with this new phase of life again marketed and commercialised by his parents. Finally the initial adulation turns sour and he becomes a figure of hate. Cousins suggested that to Christians, Tommy has a good deal to say about guilt and innocence, loneliness, exploitation and religion, though little to say about salvation.

'Miracle' is a word used as sub-heading to Michael Caine's review of the intriguing play *The Christ of Coldharbour Lane* at the Soho Theatre, London. *The Church Times*' main headline tells the story – "How a Messiah can get noticed in Brixton." It doesn't seem an easy project, but Oladipo Agboluaje has decided the Messiah would have to show people who he was, as well as tell them. The Messiah (a young man who had spent time in Brixton prison and moved into the Prisoners' Reform Programme) becomes a local hero rather than a local joke as he is witnessed miraculously restoring full physical faculties to a crippled athlete involved in a car crash.

See Me! Hear Me! is a play against global slavery, considering human trafficking to be the most heinous crime of the 21st century; apparently more profitable than selling arms. There may be other reasons for abhorrence at this trade, but in this play the essential single, shining star of eternal truth rests in Jesus. It is claimed that he brought to the whole human race the dignity of God's image.

The Donmar Warehouse production (it first played at The Centre New York in 2000) of another text by Guirgis, *Jesus Hopped the A-Train* was set in New York's City's criminal justice system. As Ben Dowell wrote in *The Stage*, "Here it takes a similarly loud, modern and unashamedly urban approach to the biblical story, turning first-century Palestine into the screech subways and cracked pavements of New York." Guirgis uses a four-letter word 25 times in his first two pages and more during a version of the Lord's Prayer as Angel Cruz struggles to remember the time-honoured words. According to reviewer Amy Barratt this foul-mouthed Broadway hit "could make you a believer." There is the attempted murder of Reverend Kim, and while it is an engaging and often absorbing play with cosmic themes discussed at street level, it fails to totally convince.

However it does stress the possible and good meaning of faith and against that the hypocrisy of those who claim to live in the Spirit. The play returned to the London stage in 2010.

In 1997 a black actor was cast as Jesus in *The Passion* play at the Park Theatre Performing Arts Centre, Union City, N.J. Death threats were received by the actor Desi Arnaz Giles. Previously the actor had taken the role of Herod and Lucifer without problems.

Jesus; The Wasted Years played at the Old Red Lion Theatre London, in 2009. Corrine Salisbury in her review considers writer Robert Meakin's set-up as one that basically anthropomorphises the gods, to give us a sub-BBC sitcom set in heaven. Jesus was played by the playwright, a "drunken waster, forever brandishing wine in a water bottle working his way through heaven's female A-list and generally bored and directionless." The play received no support from churches.

4. *I focus on some texts where the gospel story is not neglected but is subject to a degree of addition or imagination.*

Cotton Patch Gospel by Tom Key and Russell Treyez with music by Harry Chapin featured a bluegrass version of the Gospels of Matthew and John. Performed at the Wayside Theatre in Middletown USA, the musical play comprises what they describe as 'little' 30-minute stories within the bigger story of Christ's birth and resurrection. The singer-actor Ficca plays a veritable entourage of Matthew, John the Baptist, King Herod, Pontius Pilate, Caiaphas, and inevitably with no guesses asked, Jesus. There are over 40 pages of dialogue and songs. Apparently the actor walked four miles daily a month before performances began so as to be in good physical shape for this demanding multi-role playing! Jesus is born in Gainsville, and makes his way to Atlanta. Jesus tells of love's power and in a mistaken Gospel interpretation of "thou shalt love thy neighbour as thy self" the new golden rule becomes to treat others as you want to be treated. In the parable of the Good Samaritan, the good deed is done by a minority. Finally Jesus is lynched rather than hung, since this is what they do Southern style, and he rises again.

In another Guirgis play, *In Arabia We'd All Be Kings*, the character Greer talks of a Baptist past, and "The Lord" gets some mentions. There are some different, though nonethe less penetrating questions asked of God, especially how a God of mercy can create hell and withhold forgiveness. But who was responsible for Christ's ultimate betrayal? It is not Judas; it is the Jewish elder Caiaphas. It is he who hands Jesus over to Pilate. Judas feels betrayed by the Jesus he loved. He is stricken with grief. Guirgis asks our questions but they are always unsolved ones. The judge in the play bawls out, he (Judas) "betrayed the Son of God, for Christ's sake," but in a sense such a remark only goes so far and we are left to speculate what really was happening in the mind of Judas. In and amongst the many reviews it is noted that it is the character of Dowell who stresses the tender moments of insight and where the theological story is told in unadorned and human terms. Judas was played by Joseph Mawle, a slightly unfortunate choice, not for his acting, but simply because he had played Jesus in the BBC's, *The Passion* that received much publicity and gained an impressive audience. It must have been confusing to many.

Canadian Badlands Passion Play is set on the outskirts of Drumheller and has become one of the largest audience draws of any outside event in North America. To an extent it honours the medieval passion play traditions as it tells stories from the life, death and resurrection of Jesus. The organisers claim meticulous research and this includes set as well as hundreds of costumes.

The Wolverhampton Mystery Cycle is created from the texts of the actual mystery plays staged in York, Wakefield, Coventry and Chester. Whereas the originals lasted twelve hours or more, the *Wolverhampton Mystery Cycle* reduces all to two hours. It updates various aspects of the originals where the text is obscure. In this version God is female. Jesus does refer to his "Father" but only at the point where he is about to die. Jesus is played by a black actor. Original music provides a further modern backcloth.

I expected to find many plays that take on board one or more of the many fascinating aspects of the Gospel story, but outside of the major works already mentioned, they either do not exist or have escaped my notice. Obviously there are many texts; sketches and short plays written specifically for churches and often for presentation during a worship service. I look for a stage play that has the insight and innocence that I found in Pasolini's film *Gospel of Matthew*. In recent time my viewing highlight has been the presentation of *The Mysteries* at the National. It came with a wonderful set of actors, musicians and dancers, and not least on the A plus list the overall concept in design and lighting. It was memorable.

5   *Inter-faith plays are few and far between,*
    however I discovered several.

In 2005, Berlin's Spiritdialox Theatre, in the quarter of Berlin-Mitte, staged an unusual theatre project *Jesus and Mohammed*. While the title may well pass many people by there were those who saw it as provocative and the usual protests followed. Controversially this play was cast for two women, although out of respect for Islamic beliefs, the actresses never optically slide into the role of Mohammed, but direct their focus on his sacred texts.

The director Alexander Korp said the idea was to take original texts and blend them together, and allowing them to be spoken by the female performer, without an exact distinction being directly noticeable. He adds, "When is it a text from the Koran, and when is it from the Bible? A debate, a kind of conversational quarrel, then develops between the actresses." He speaks about the poetry and beauty of the texts, "Only when they are spoken by a woman, one more component comes into being than one is accustomed to and expects. This creates irritation." Hence "We do not play Jesus and Mohammed; an actor portrays the archangel Gabriel and an actress Mohammed. But it is very obvious that they are neither Mohammed nor the archangel Gabriel."

Liberating Jesus, a one man play by Leonard Jackson, and premiered in Santa Monica, California, managed to bring

East and West together, with Christianity, Judaism and Islam brought into alignment. Traditional Christians were warned by the reviewer to stay away as the writer ventured into suggesting that Jesus shows the "Oneness at the heart of all paths and traditions." Jackson has Jesus explaining how the stories of his life and death have been misunderstood.

Less expected, and somewhat disappointing in its execution, was Hanif Kureishi's stage play *The Black Album*. This was based on his second novel of the same name. The central thrust of this morality play focuses on the dilemma of the Muslim student who could be tempted into pleasure seeking and so turn his back on the seeming demands of his religion. This would see him forsaking those who would insist on strict interpretations of its practice, and Islamic brothers who approve of their women veiled and obedient. It made its foray into theatre at the Cottesloe, National Theatre, in London during the late summer of 2009.

6. *There are plays and musicals with scripture allusions and a reliance on gospel and spiritual songs. There are plays where the story is set in a church or chapel.*

Who can forget Nicola Hughes' playing to great effect Zarita in the musical *Simply Heavenly*? It was not so much about religious expression as about the bad days of Harlem. It had a brilliantly imagined set by Rob Howell. In the early part of 1996, London's Cambridge Theatre rang with an upbeat gospel of hope with its presentation of *Mama, I Want to Sing*. There are plenty of gospel and church references and if there was a message then it came in the quasi-religious song 'Faith can move mountains'. The lyrics were ordinary, the singing divine. It was the first stage outing for soul-gospel singer Chaka Khan who played the church's "Choice diva" – the Queen bee. In talking about the popular production before it began at London's Cambridge Theatre she said, "It's a very familiar story in the gospel church, the rise of a singer from gospel choir to chart success, where the star singer gets offers from nightclubs and record companies, and the big dilemmas about whether to sing for God or the masses – and the church and family have to decide whether to accept it."

James Baldwin's *The Amen Corner* first premiered in 1954 with its theme tracing the walk between sinfulness and righteousness. It also questions about the love for God and family and which should come first. It is set on a Sunday morning in Harlem and begins with a church service. In the early 1960s it ran with considerable success at London's Lyric Theatre, then a Stoll Moss Theatre.

As with his novel *Go Tell It on The Mountain* written in 1952 both rely on black spirituals and biblical allusions. They were part of what has been called Baldwin's "come-to-Jesus-stuff". Here was caught something of the influence black fundamentalist/Pentecostal expression had upon his formative years and eventual unease with "the suffocating 'safety' of religion."

Newcastle's Live Theatre in a co-production with the National produced *The Pitmen Painters* with its text that gave a vision of spirituality and hope. Martin Warner, Canon Treasurer at St Paul's Cathedral, thought the Church might well identity with the vision of human flourishing which is found in the play. The themes of common interest are good news about the scope of being human, refreshment from the tyranny of commerce that mortgages our time.

Doubt: A Parable arrived at London's fringe Tricycle Theatre. Heavy with accolades from across the Atlantic and a Pulitzer Prize, it carried the topical theme of child abuse in the Catholic Church. It seemed ponderous, and Fiona Mountford wrote in *The London Evening Standard* (November 27, 2007) that it was "a disappointment."

Blues for Mister Charlie from James Baldwin is set in a small southern town in the USA and deals with racial tension and conflict. We meet the congregation of the Rev. Henry's church. During this engrossing play there is a fascinating conversation between Parnell and the Rev. Phelps on religion and race.

And Jesus Moonwalks the Mississippi by Marcus Gardley was premiered in 2010. The Cutting Ball Theatre's production is set in the context of the American Civil War and is set on the banks of the Mississippi. It is described as a poetic journey of forgiveness and redemption. Traditional storytelling, gospel music and humour create "a rich, imaginative world that allows trees to preach, rivers to waltz, and Jesus to moonwalk." He recalls his grandmother singing spirituals and praying. She would also tell beautiful stories. It was this that led him to write this new play. The writer Marcus Gardley is a multiple award-winning poet-playwright with many awards and nominations.

Gospel at Colonus is a musical that is a reworking of the ancient Greek playwright's tragedy *Oedipus at Colonus*. It was presented at the Edinburgh Festival 2010. Just previous to this visit the production had been staged at New York's Lincoln Centre, but its actual beginnings go back to presentation at a workshop on the Fringe in 1982. A Pentecostal preacher narrates, historic Gospel groups, The Blind Boys of Alabama, The Soul Stirrers and the inspirational Voices of the Abyssinian Baptist Church in Harlem sing.

7. There are several plays that have been built around the life of a prominent Christian.

The recent main benefactor has been Dietrich Bonhoeffer, the German theologian. Bonhoeffer belonged to the Confessing Church who in part plotted to remove Hitler. He was hanged shortly before the Second World War ended. While at one time the darling of the religious liberals and possibly of the left – along with another German, Moltmann – Bonhoeffer in more recent time has gained himself a fairly conservative theological market. In 2005, *Candles in the Window* was presented to commemorate his sixtieth anniversary. Just hours before his execution he had written to the Anglican Bishop George Bell, "This is the end, but for me the beginning of life."

It was given its world premiere by Bellehurst Productions. Written by the American Christian playwright Kathleen Ann Thompson the play was set in the waiting room of Victoria Station, London. A Jewish woman, a refugee from Hitler's Germany, is waiting for the boat train that will take back to her homeland. She meets an American woman who wears a widow's black. They realise that each of them has a particular call on Bonhoeffer. The German Jewish woman was the Bonhoeffer's family maid, the American a widow of a British Secret Service officer imprisoned with him. In his review Bill Dunlop felt the writer served up an awful lot of Bonhoeffer's theology, "largely through passages cut and pasted into the mouths of the two characters without a personal context". He saw the play as a preachy polemic, "something one hopes Bonhoeffer himself would have demurred at. What's worse, we quickly lose the thread of some of the arguments, as the play flits from personal to political and then elsewhere."

One of the church's most perceptive commentators, Brian Cooper in the *Baptist Times* (August 25th 2005) thought it superbly performed. Cooper is a theologian and biblical commentator in his own right and once edited *The British Weekly*. For him the play revels in a man "supremely committed in utter trust to the victory of Christ in this world and the next. This conviction sustained his deep immersion as a Christian in public affairs to the every end." The play was performed on the 60th anniversary of his death, 2006.

In 2008 in Hollywood's Advent Theatre, A.L. Staggs presented his one character play *A View from the Underside: The Legacy of Dietrich Bonhoeffer*. From his prison cell Bonhoeffer writes about his struggles with evil, injustice and God. He wrestles with how to live by your faith in a world that may kill you for it.

In a different kind of way and context the various works of Dario Fo have upset many within Church and government circles in Italy, so much so that his one-man show *Giotto a Non Giotto* about the famous cycle of Giotto wall paintings in the Basilica, Assisi based on the life of St Francis, was stopped by the city's Bishop.

Fo speaks of a long-time love for the life of St Francis and it led him writing a one-man show in 1999. *Francis, the Holy Jester* staged at Edinburgh's Pleasance Theatre August 2009, under the new title *Francis, the Holy Jester*. (The medieval 'guillari' or jesters once entertained in the market square, singing, dancing and telling a story that often had a lurking message. Fo sees a humane Christ, "one on the side of the underdogs, and possessing a pagan, almost Dionysiac joy for love, festivity, beauty and worldly things". At the same time he is full of hatred and violence toward those who misuse religion and who in their own arrogance crush the weak and forgotten. In terms of St. Francis and *Francis, the Holy Jester* we are brought into the presence of someone who he sees as a true follower of Christ, for some Christians can be hypocritical and greedy. A heading of "Admiration for a 'true Christian' " prefaces an extremely good article in the *Church Times*, by the writer Katy Hounsell-Robert.

Many will remember the film *The Song of Bernadette* starring Jennifer Jones, an American actress of disturbing beauty, and who died late 2009. Unwisely there was an attempt by some well- meaning folk to bring the story of Bernadette to the West End stage. Considerable monies were spent but that did not prevent the show closing within days.

The Edinburgh Festival in 2007 gave space to the one woman show *St Catherine of Siena*, a Tuscan saint who died 630 years ago; *The Cost of Freedom* focuses on the founding of the African Methodist Church in the USA by Richard Allen. The British Olivier Award for 2010 was given to a young American playwright Katori Hall for her play *Mountaintop*. Although it had several readings in various parts of her homeland, US theatre groups expressed little interest and voiced concerns about its content. However the two person production found a home in Britain that eventually meant the Trafalgar Studios, London. The text centres around the night before Dr Martin Luther King Jnr was murdered.

Martin Luther King Jnr was named by his parents after the great 16th century religious reformer from Germany, Martin Luther (Luter in German). John Osborne's play *Luther* was premiered at Nottingham Playhouse in 1961. Albert Finney masterfully created the role with the production finding its London life at the Royal Court Theatre, and St. James Theatre on Broadway, New York. The pivotal moment comes when Luther's long suffered constipation that entailed hours sitting on the jake ends when he realises that the central tenet of Christian faith rests in 'justification by faith' – that salvation is given by God's good grace and is not earned either by paying indulgences or in acts of faith.

8. *I bring into play a number of texts that have a religious underpinning or at least make use of religious ideas.*

It seems likewise sacrilegious not to mention the continuously successful work of David Hare. His play *Gethsemane* (2008) may give a hint to the unwary that it is a study of Jesus' last moments before crucifixion or more specifically a play about the betrayal of Jesus. It is not, but the betrayal aspect is worked through political corruption and the lack of vision beyond the self-consideration of those who beat their chests and profess to want a better world, and one that in the end largely favours them. At some depth the same writer wrote *The Judas Kiss* (1998) which centres on the somewhat torrid life of Oscar Wilde, the last in a trilogy of plays about love and betrayal. The word-play on this rests in the title as it recalls one of the original twelve disciples of Jesus who for thirty pieces of silver betrayed Jesus, with a kiss to identify him to those who wished eventually to take his life.

Racing Demons by David Hare bounces off the famous line of David Inge that "The church that is married to the spirit of the age will be a widow in the next." *Racing Demons* (was the first of a trilogy in which the writer looks at British institutions. The playwright has stated that his intention was not to theorize but to portray the lives of individuals trying to survive within them.

The play is set in South London 1992, at a time in British history when the Church of England was divided over the issue of women's ordination. The Tory government castigated the Church for its lack of support. The play centres on a group of Anglican clergyman who are trying to make sense of their work in South London. Naturally there are all kinds of differences within the group in their attitude to the Church, to Jesus, their faith, and ways of conducting their ministry.

Angels in America played the Lyric, Hammersmith, London in the summer of 2007, although it made its first stage entry in the early 1990s. This is a two-part, seven hour epic, and so not to be taken lightly. It springs off the crisis and confusion of Reagan's reign and throws into it a grand humanist vision. The demonic figure of Roy Cohn, Senator McCarthy's former henchman discovers political power does not stem the possibility of terminal illness. As Michael Billington writes in his *Guardian* newspaper review: "Above them hovers an angel of death, who argues that a planet abandoned by God can only survive through stasis. This play with its mix of fantasy and realism travels a fascinating journey and suggests at its end that failed and corrupt political systems are 'still humanly perfectible'."

The Cottesloe auditorium at the National Theatre, London, presented *Love the Sinner*, a new play by Drew Pautz early summer 2010. The initial setting is night; a hotel conference room. Worthy Anglican leaders lay and clerical, and a token earnest woman, involve themselves in one of those roundabout discussions instantly recognizable as a talk shop that goes nowhere as everyone scurries to find agreement, however bland, and if so, imagine they have achieved much. The play has a number of issues; including an attempt to clarify the Church's attitude towards gay people. We meet Joseph, the hotel porter, an evangelical, who is gay. There is much more. As Michael Billington said in his *Guardian* review there are "a number of big issues: clerical schism, marital hypocrisy, patronizing attitudes to the developing world. Pautz's target is public and private evasiveness. Refreshing as it is to find religious issues getting a theatrical airing, I wish the play had some of the intellectual sinew of *Racing Demon*." With that, there is agreement.

In 2003, the National Theatre staged a dramatization of Philip Pullman's *His Dark Materials*, which drew comment from Norman Lebrecht in the *London Evening Standard* that here was an intelligent piece of anti-Christian propaganda masquerading as children's entertainment.

The original Broadway production of *Rent* played London's Shaftsbury Theatre (home to *Hair*) in May 1998 for some fifteen months. 2001 and again in 2002, it played The Prince of Wales at the heart of London's theatre-land before arriving at London's Duke of York in 2003. Soul, gospel and blues provided a musical backcloth while the text toured the minds of a community of young New Yorkers, and celebrated among other things the power of love.

The Last Confession at the Theatre Royal, Haymarket was less on Jesus and more on the battle of worldly glory and less religious faith, and set in the imagined corridors of Vatican power. For actors it shone, thanks to a remarkable playing of Cardinal Benelli by David Suchet.

More controversial is *Rent Boy Ave: A Fairy's Tale*. The 2008 production centres on the activities of two guys – Mark a veteran of male prostitution since the age of 17 and a new kid on the street, David. The two struggle to survive the nasty world of which they are a part. There is even a fairy godmother nun, Sister Mercy, who quite apart from fish-net wearing knows the art of Bible-thumping. Theirs is the search for self-meaning and salvation.

The inventive Cornish company Kneehigh played at the Olivier Theatre, National Theatre during May 2007 in a stage version of the classic British film *A Matter of Life And Death* that was directed by the adventurous Emma Rice. There are Kneehigh alterations from the film text, but we remain, as the *Church Times* reviewer Michael Caines describes, with the love story. Squadron Leader Peter Carter speaks to June, an American radio operator, but a brief moment before bailing out of his burning aeroplane. Carter survives. The other crewmembers do not. Heaven is not happy. Carter should have died. He has to prove why he deserves to live. It makes for a fascinating story and stage play.

There are plays based on the literary work of C.S. Lewis that have found great success, especially in the United States; *The Screwtape Letters* ran for many months on Broadway in 2007 and ended a run at The Mercury Theatre, Chicago, in the spring of 2009. Thousands have seen *The Lion King* and for some Christians its text has direct bearing on how they interpret areas of Scripture, especially those that deal with the 'end' of things.

Seemingly opposite to the shouts of Faith triumphant, and hands raised in the air to say that "God is so good to me" there is Sarah Kane who took her life in her late twenties. Her plays, *Blasted / Phaedra's Love / Cleansed / Crave* and *4.48 Psychosis* would not be viewed well in church circles – unfortunately. She fired words with deadly rapidity as she raced into the subject of death or a distaste for life that surely echoes some of the most riveting Old Testament passages. Her writing is akin to having your skin pulled off to reveal the rawness underneath; or in human lives to tear away the up-front surface that all is well to then find the grief, and horror; the desertion of inner humanity and sanctity. Yet you feel you wished you could have told her that there are people who care, who do embrace and hug with a warmth and commitment, who do feel the pain but know that light emerges through the darkness like day from night. Interestingly she absorbed Beckett and T.S. Eliot, and drew inspiration from Auschwitz and Kosovo. She could have tried the Old Testament book of Lamentations.

The Death of the Black Jesus has only loose connotations with the theme of this book. The play by David Barr was premiered at the union Theatre, Kansas as *Betrayal of the Black Jesus*. The director Cynthia Levin won the National Players' Award. In the play a local TV presenter has invited three former members of a radical Panther group of the 1960s into the studio. The play examines racial attitudes.

Berkhoff's *Harry's Christmas* at the Donmar Theatre in 1985 is a moving one man play that is both amusing and sad. Berkoff writes: "Harry is one of those whom the buffets of the world has left stranded on a barren shore and he is dealing with it for the last time, but it is an amalgam of many of us." Harry is well into his observations before he finds his thoughts centering on the Christ Child. At this point Harry recalls Jesus saying, "Suffer the little children to come unto me" and adds, "I'm one of them... I'm a child of his."

Shaw's play *Major Barbara* was revived at the National Theatre, London, early 2008, with Nicholas Hytner directing. Wealth, the arms trade, poverty and Christianity come under scrutiny. Tomi Alayi reviewed the production for *The Methodist Recorder;* "the text is an exploration of one of life's most complex moral issues, the real meaning of right and wrong." The play's main character Barbara Undershaft is an enthusiastic member of the Salvation Army and while the overall debate applies generally it is very much an ever present dilemma for a Christian organization that is dependent on raising money for its continuance. It too may be faced with the dilemma as to whether it accepts a large amount of what is in the end 'dirty money'. It may argue that it would make better use of that money rather than leaving it to be spent by the immoral accumulator.

Presented by the Katselas Theatre Company in Los Angeles, The Jesus Hickey is a modern day fable revolving around the seduction of celebrity. In the play the daughter of a tough Irish labourer discovers a hickey on her neck and it is shaped in the image of Jesus. The pilgrims arrive.

9. Here, I take in a little of the classical field and its focus on Jesus.

Several examples come immediately to mind. There is Messiaen's thought on the *Incarnation of Jesus*. Robert Beale, reviewer in *The Manchester Evening News*, mentions Messiaen's *La Nativite Du Seigneur*, and the movement '*Jesus accepte la Souffrance*' that says much about the Cross and the doctrine of redemption. In Jonathan Rathbone's *Requiem for the Condemned Man* we have excerpts from the Lord's Prayer and the Pie Jesu; we almost travel into a Passion narrative. In John Taverner's *Fall and Resurrection* two large choirs, a large orchestra, the great organ and the bells of St Paul's, and a biblical patchwork text by his mentor Mother Thekla produced 70 minutes of wondrous word and sound. Fiona Maddocks, *The Observer Review*, 9 January, 2000, reminds us of Taverner's volubly declared hatred of art music (music written for the concert hall rather than for God) and how this has set him apart from his fellow composers "who at once scorn and envy him".

In America the celebrated composer-lyricist Walter Robinson noted for his lyrical song 'Harriet Tubman' won awards for his *Look What A Wonder Jesus Has Done*. Later he win much praise for Moses, considered by the *New York Times* as a "celebration of freedom".

There is much that is clear and beautifully told in the Gospels, whether seen as factual or simply human words that tell a story concealing hidden teaching. Yet without wishing to give the impression that I am some kind of literalist there are those moments when a writer either has not read the text of scripture carefully or fondly imagines he can improve upon it, or a director thinks the change makes for a better moment. Such seems to be the case in the 2009 staging by the English National Opera of Handel's *Messiah*. *The Church Times* reviewer tells of how he found unexpectedly moving the announcement of the angel to Mary that she has been chosen to bear the "child of childs" and so she is transformed by joy into a happy and radiant mother. However that is a distortion of Scripture and belongs in the writer's imagination, and those watching and hearing may assume its factual nature. What is worse is not so much a misreading of the Gospel story, beautiful or not in the ENO production, but simply an ever more tender and moving story has been missed.

The angel may have told Mary to rejoice, but she did not. Somehow she kept all these things in her heart. There comes the day when she decides to visit her aunt Elizabeth. We have this powerful image of the unborn Jesus carried in the womb of a young girl who walks through endless villages, concealing a time-bomb within her but she tells nobody. When she meets with an also pregnant Elizabeth it is the baby in the aunt's womb that kicks on sensing the unborn baby Jesus, and it is only then that the fireworks explode and Mary rejoices.

I did appreciate Deborah Warner's picture of a today's Mary slumped in front of the television set surrounded by ordinary furniture, who with some surprise finds her bed covered in lillies and receives the angel's news. That said, and some would say not so interesting, I suspect a Mary of today would not be slavishly running through the TV channels. There has to be a sense of someone who carries youthful wonder, a fascination with the rituals of Jewish practice, with a youthful sense of purity and innocence. Maybe she loves smells and stars, wind and trees, who marvels even if sometimes disturbed at the changes of her own body.

Warner is no stranger to Christian material. In 2000 there was her semi-staging of *St John The Passion* for the English National Opera. Mark Padmore sang the Evangelist, the omnipresent figure who relates the sacred narrative; he speaks of the work addressing suffering at its deepest level. It deals with the issue of what it is to feel pain, physical and psychological, what it is to lose a loved one. It's trying to make sense of the terrible things that happen in our lives. So, we see the suffering Christ, so too the human aspect of Peter's denial of Christ.

Another outstanding director is Katie Mitchell whose setting in 2007 of Bach's *St. Matthew Passion* in the aftermath of the Dunblane school massacre caused much controversy. At Glyndebourne she was invited to turn the famous religious piece into an opera. Jonathan Miller had taken the same piece in 1993.

Mitchell told Paul Taylor of *The Independent* that she was aware of how much the piece meant to both Christian and non-Christian. From this comment it is apparent that she was well aware how her work has sharply divided theatre people into the camp that says her work has imaginative rigour and others who find it oppressive and pretentious. Taylor says she managed to conquer her qualms and created a "production that characteristically goes for broke". And why not? It is this quality that is lacking from most contemporary versions of the Jesus story. Jesus on stage cries out for directors who are not overwhelmed by the need to bow to the religious constituency. However it is also an inhibiting factor for some actors who often find it hard not to imbue their characters with what they perceive to be the right religious framework, as they unconsciously sink into an odd reverence.

Each member of the Glyndebourne chorus was given a character, "whose individual experience of grief psychologically motivates their behaviour during the course of their work". Asked why she chose to set the piece in a community struggling to come to terms with the loss of children she says it came from conversation with the tenor Mark Padmore. "He pointed out that, of Bach's 20 children, 11 died before him, 10 of those in infancy. We felt that on some level this is being written out here."

The ending sounds more like a lullaby than a funeral. The programme notes by Karen Armstrong remind us that in the *St. Matthew Passion* there are only hints of Jesus' resurrection. The words of the final chorus say: "We sit down in tears and call/To Thee in the tomb:/Rest softly, softly rest". Paul Taylor says there is no false sense of what we would now describe as "closure" so it makes for an almost "unbearably moving and dignified conclusion" to Mitchell's opera, as the parents lay flowers and candles on the makeshift shrine, and get ready to leave. Consolation, but not catharsis: the effect of the *St Mathew Passion* on these characters is too complex to be tidied up in the word "therapy".

A further brief 'opera' reference must be to *The Last Supper* by Harrison Birtwistle. The underlying story is simple but effective, namely you take the original gathering of Jesus and his disciples as described in the Gospels but you ask what it might be if a second chance were permitted. In terms of Judas there is an engaging question mark hovering over the proceedings as to whether or not he has been invited. However, he arrives and in musical terms adds his voice to their singing of 'Amen'. Jesus similarly arrives without fanfare and, as described by Fiona Maddocks in *The Observer* April 23 2000, "He atones for the disciples' sins, washing their feet one by one," and at this moment in some style he recites a litany of Man's crimes over the past 2000 years.

I also mention in passing the Christian and religious influence of Shakesperian text; after all, *Hamlet* has been described as a Christian play in a pagan universe. And is not Lear during the text so near to the Jesus of the Gospels? John Pridmore in an excellent article in the *Church Times* (June 22, 2007), "What Lear says about the Church reminds us of Christ whose incarnation and crucifixion are the great acts of divine investiture." Pridmore toward the end of his powerful discourse sees the model of the future Church held up by King Lear as, "one of a Church that regroups outside the gates, in that wilderness where the only shelter is beneath the bare branches of a cross, where rare but lovely flowers grow, the virtue we see blossoming in the exchange of charity between a broken king and his companion in the storm."

10. Final Thoughts

While I have been intrigued that there have been so many plays in recent time that have touched upon Jesus there is nonetheless the feeling that few have achieved real depth.

Some derive from the prevailing cultural norms of our time. Until recently few would have dared to suggest Jesus might have been gay. These days it gives cause for no surprise, although some of the texts I have mentioned would not find a welcome reception in say Penzance or Inverness.

I am aware of the inherent problems for the playwright who comes to texts variously interpreted not just by scholars but also by other cultures.

Malachi Martin in his book *Jesus Now* talks of the unfortunate but inevitable coming together of verbose Jews, mentalistic Greeks and the heavily logical Latins to muddy things. And so have come millions of words and miles of paper. Martin talks of the tags that became attached to Jesus and expressed in polysyllabic terms, composite phrase, holy shibboleths and technical terms – what he calls "the legal tender in the divine commerce of religion and authority. To come of course the brooding domes of Western thought. Jesus became a definable entity, known by his doctor's cap and his teacher's colours. The wonder is that the Word was not smothered completely."

Setting aside many issues, the Jesus seen at various times in history is altogether a much more radical figure than many playwrights acknowledge. I have the feeling that too many religious people desire play scripts portraying Jesus as a pleasant young man who every now and then said something sensible or useful, but who is hardly the figure that has dominated so much of the world's art form expressions. I simply ask how can there be bread for humankind unless plays on Jesus disturb or shock, as with the Jesus that drove Martin Luther King (himself with various weaknesses and temptations) to achieve a massive change in American racial attitudes.

I am not suggesting fringe and lightweight texts should not exist and that all texts must stir or awaken, but conflict is the essence of drama. This reminds me of an exchange between the American Presidential hopeful Harry Truman and a supporter who urged him to, "Give 'em hell, Harry." Truman replied, "I didn't give 'em hell. I tell the truth and it sounds like hell."

I am not too sure what kind of depth charges a famed playwright such as Mark Ravenhill might drop if given the Gospels as his project but one thing is certain, hundreds would gather with banners, the media would be inundated with protests, for as Michael Kustow has said, Ravenhill's characters are, "ready to put up their sexual identities up for grabs".

Murray Watts the playwright and theatre director, told readers of *Artyfact*, the magazine of the national Arts Centre Group, that "You can only fail in dramatising the life of Jesus, but you can try to fail in the best and most moving way possible." Watts was speaking as scriptwriter for the animated film *The Miracle Maker* which dealt with aspects of Jesus' life. Yet perhaps the playwright can find empathy with Luther who insists upon Christ's historic life and works, and that those who desire to seek him "in some private way" betray him afresh: he must be sought "as He was and walked on earth."

CHAPTER SIX

An Interval

This short chapter asks whether the playwright actually instigates change or reflects an overall existing and shifting mood. For a brief examination of this in terms of the book's subject I return to the lengthy chapter that began with *Jesus Christ Superstar* and during its journey focussed on *Godspell*, the other religious styled musical that grabbed audiences in the early 1970s. Both texts continue in performance from the professional to the amateur.

The 1960s had passed. Society was certainly in flux. Young people continued to pursue their desire to do things their way. The consumer world was ever readying itself to follow whatever made the cash registers ring. Prosperity beckoned for Western countries. Music assumed a more peaceful pose after the rampant high energy, drug-ridden surges of the latter part of the sixties. Secular musical styles were creeping into general Christian consciousness, modern translations of the Bible became almost the norm, although the use of the vernacular in pop-ridden religious songs was sadly lacking. It was the tune that carried the day, for many of the words were as incomprehensible as the ancient Christian liturgies.

In his book *The Sounds of the Sixties and the Church* Stephen Wright concludes his fascinating survey by saying that unless the Church is happy to remain a cultural backwater, removed and apart from any semblance of contemporary life, it needs to change. That was true then; sadly to some degree, this remains the case today.

My immediate question is whether some aspects of change were already afoot or the germ of such was alive sufficiently to respond to the two musicals. Malachi Martin considered the two productions together in their depiction of Jesus on stage. Both knocked the stuffing out of reverence. "Remember we were always told to be pure and wholesome and clean? That innocence was best? That you have to be quiet and reverential, sit up straight and talk clearly and go about your business seriously and maturely? Well, forget it. It is time to be liberated". (ibid p. 116).

Godspell in particular encouraged, as *Hair* had done earlier, the sense that one could sprawl on sofa and floor to sing and pray the faith; humour was in fashion. It was a time to laugh. Happiness was no longer considered such a serious matter for Jesus. Jesus the Superstar was not on Mount Tabor ready to remind people of their failings and the need to cleanse their souls. Neither was he on Calvary bleeding on a cross, nor prowling the Vatican, or calling a point of order at the Methodist Conference. He was as Malachi Martin so sweetly put it, "right on top of a huge phallus made of wood and paper and glue and paint, centre stage. Not as big as Mickey Mouse in Disneyland, but certainly as homely as Peanuts, and as regular as Archie Bunker. You felt as though you had known the guy all your life."

Clergy and lay people may preach endless sermons, but who is to say that the thousands bussed into London's West End remember more the visual and dramatic direction than the words so lovingly enunciated day by day in performance. Whatever the case, at that moment in time both musicals made the Church seem somnolent and tiresome. For the Church the question could have been, 'What has all this to do with Jesus of Nazareth?" It either had no answer or it simply wanted to appear relevant and so jump on the bandwagon and become even more irrelevant. Although, as the next chapter suggests, the two productions did let loose within the Christian community musical projects that were aimed to correct the apparently false teaching of *JCS* in particular.

Certainly, Jesus undergoes a new emphasis. He is hardly the mind-denying doctor of the elaborate nature of medieval Faith, but perhaps that is to choose a description for effect against the Sixties liberal Protestant feeling that "Jesus is one the boys." However, in much of the 'praise' and 'trendy' lore of unhappy priests and ministers chasing acceptance if Jesus is one of the boys, then decades on we can greet God as super-dad, all friendly and cuddly and wanting to be invited to a worship service, or at least thanked for coming. By 2006 Jesus has become an unpaid ad. boy. The Churches Advertising Network (CAN) linking up with the website of the secular youth forum, *myspace.com,* have brought Jesus into the arena of alcohol boozing. Jesus's face can be seen in an empty beer glass with the accompanying words, "Where will you find him?" Not it seems in a good glass of Ruddles or St Austell brewers but by linking into 'myspace' and from there following directions to the rejesus.co.uk website where information is given about the faith, plus links to churches. According to the *Church Times* of 15th September,2006 a spokesperson for CAN explained that there was a "media preoccupation for finding images of Jesus in everything from egg yolks to current buns." And to think it was not even the first of April...

As a final footnote to this chapter, I am conscious of the danger posed by our subject title, for like most subjects, it is misleading to view things in isolation. The productions described were certainly not the only interesting theatre works, indeed if we take in general theatre of the early 1960s then we move into plays from Harold Pinter, Arnold Wesker, John Osborne, Joan Littlewood, Weiss and Camus. not forgetting Mort Sahl and Lenny Bruce, English satire in *Beyond The Fringe* vein.

During this period I could be found on many an evening up in the 'gods' and falling in love with theatre. However, in *The Observer* 18 September 1960, the great theatre critic Kenneth Tynan decrying the state of English theatre, considering it to be in a state of deadlock. He judged the audiences to be pre-dominantly conservative, wedded by age and habit to the old standards. As for the younger playwrights, "they were predom-inantly anti-conservative, irretrievably divorced from the ideo-logical status quo." Obviously they need a new audience, but in order to attract it they will have to define and dramatise the new values for which they generally stand.

CHAPTER SEVEN

Christians And Churches Cast Jesus On Stage

The very title of this chapter tells a story. It suggests there is a bevy of dramatic material presented within churches, but not heard on the general stage. This may be because it is not good enough to penetrate beyond religious confines or simply that there is at present a bias existing against Christian content, or even that it lacks the desired commercial element. It is also the case that Christians may wish to celebrate in dramatic form various events in their history that fail to resonate with general society.

On the other hand why should writers not provide material for particular constituencies, offer texts to predetermined areas? People write religious books, produce films and videos and no one questions that, so why not drama? There are some theatre clubs and specialised venues where playwrights present political, moral and social diatribes. No one complains. More important is the question, does the text touch a nerve or two?

I admit this particular chapter strays into a general description of theatre companies which have to some extent a Christian orientation. There is the assumption that lying behind whatever is said and done there exists the desire for a further understanding of Jesus. Obviously there is considerable difference in emphasis. Church drama of a kind has always been present, but more recently this has run with the changing nature of popular culture. It has brought to the fore a number of enterprising drama groups previously operating on some kind of professional basis, but facing financial difficulties, save a few with monetary support from the more fundamentalist wing of some American churches. It is slightly dangerous to name names.

However at the outset it seems reasonable to confront those who in no way would admit Jesus on centre stage into their buildings, let alone any secular setting.

Some of their thinking is encapsulated in an article in *The Evangelical Times*, August, 1992. The author of this piece Billy Morrison sees drama as simply entertainment, and that applies to pre-Reformation Mystery plays or modern drama. He sees the proponents of religious subject drama often do what they do by way of evangelizing their age. He questions this assertion. He asks, "Why do the unsaved go to watch drama? Because they want to hear the gospel or because they enjoy acting? If the drama and mime were replaced with straightforward preaching of the Gospel from the word of God, how many of these people would continue to attend the service?" In the first place, whatever the motive he ought to be pleased that what he calls the 'unsaved' are actually on church premises. Secondly whatever their motive it is possible for it to be circumvented by what they see; after watching a Jasperian Theatre Company production a whole family linked up with the church where we were presenting material, because what they saw and heard moved them on to deeper things.

Thirdly even within the context of how he envisages Christian presentation, there have been variable shifts of emphasis. I rather think Morrison confuses the centrality of pulpit and pulpit oratory with how the Faith has been celebrated century after century. It has not been about the persuasive and powerful verbal utterance, yet as my co-writer has already mentioned, preaching and expounding the Word of God has its own dramatic form. There is such a thing as body language, as well as the dramatic use of glasses and other props. Maybe ensuring the head has a wonderful crop of whiter-than-white hair to enhance the impression of our being in the presence of a distinguished person. A carefully cultivated beard may emphasise the sense of possible profundity coming our way!

Fourthly as is evident from Pauline and other Epistles, while the Faith was strong and vibrant, it was subject to being tailored in presentation to the audiences addressed.

Fifthly it might be construed from the New Testament that true evangelism is a one to one encounter and is not about vast assemblies aided by the dramatic input of choir, soloists, testimonies and altar calls.

Sixthly, in any church or gospel hall there is already drama present in the intrinsic layout and design. The New Testament does not lay down the theological, spiritual and architectural possibilities.

Seventhly, the voice and projection of preacher or Bible expositor will have an influence on how that Word is received. A repetitive and dull voice will hinder. In any case it has been plainly evident to anyone who hears many preachers and speakers that many adopt a received and given style. The use of the voice is drama.

Mr Morrison is right in saying that the Scriptures at various times have been kept from the people retained as sole province of the clergy. But it quite another thing to say that in pre-Reformation days the word of God is replaced by a poor imitation. It is to forget that at one time there were no printing presses. It is to forget that at one time many could neither read nor write. The Faith was presented visually and in the mystery play enacted before their very eyes.

Morrison ends his feature by pointing out the mighty work of God in the great revivals of the last three hundred or so years and recalls affectionate names such as Whitfield, the Wesleys, Jonathan Edwards and C.H. Spurgeon. Who would doubt their testimony to Jesus, but equally it seems beyond dispute that they themselves were great dramatic showmen for God. Did all people come and listen to them with the sole motive of wanting to hear the Bible explained or were they like people of old who came racing out into the streets to hear this man from Nazareth because everyone was talking about him and his fame was spreading abroad?

I have spent time on this feature simply because the writer is saying much that resonates with folk in general. In considering Jesus on Centre Stage there has to be an awareness of the strong possibility of confusion in some quarters.

Confusion over motive, purpose and method of those of us who write and work in dramatic fields and at the same time express an allegiance to the Lordship of Christ. I am constantly asked how I can work in theatre and still profess to being a Christian. It is a question that drives me near to the edge of sanity but at the same time I have to learn to respect what lies behind it.

The tenor of this author is simple, although some Christians involved in drama would not share it. I suggest that there is no such thing as Christian drama – there is drama, period. Within the parameters of drama, the world is an empty stage. It is there. It is there as a form that should be understood for its own disciplines and methods, although these may change from one decade to the next, and indeed there are countless variations and schools of thought.

In fairness to Morrison his views were very much those expressed in conservative evangelical circles during the 1970s when theatre was considered the Devils' domain. Writing in 1992 Deidre Ducker in *The Cut* believes Rookmaaker, Schaeffer and the national Arts Centre Group opened our eyes to what she calls, "our God-given creativity." So like frogs spawning, it appears that every church boasts a music/drama group. On this she comments: "Yet the complete commitment of secular amateur dramatic groups is rarely achieved by Christian amateurs – who tend to feel that if the message is right everything else will fall into place – effortlessly." Ducker's own background has taken her through every level of theatre surveying smaller theatre companies both secular and religious. Her words in 1992 have an even more potent ring in the 21st century; all theatres suffer from similar constraints: lack of time, space, money.

Hence anyone involved in drama should first strive to acknowledge its own innate wonder, and be aware that the dramatic text presented can carry all kinds of messages. There may be plays that are overtly religious in subject matter, some specifically Christian or Bible-based. Equally there are plays that adopt an anti-religious slant, usually choosing some aspect of Christian faith or some dubious aspect of Church expression. However no-one speaks of agnostic or atheistic drama. The drama has to live by the quality of writing, acting, directing and sometimes by costume and set; hopefully by an inter-weaving of all aspects. Equally so the actor who says he is a Christian is not a better actor per se than someone who is not.

Nor is there any truth in imagining that if someone prays hard enough or engages a group of believers to pray for him that he will be promoted from playing two minutes and five words in a play at St Barnabas Church to playing Hamlet at the National. It seems too much like a record of long ago where a young boy called Sparkey dreamt he could suddenly sit at a piano and engage with some of the most difficult music pieces imaginable. It was a lovely dream.

Of course there will be audiences attuned to particular forms, and in the Christian world it is too often the desire to see things wrapped up conveniently for them, requiring no thought. Equally some prefer to hear words that make them feel good, confirm them in their feelings. In one sense it is reasonable when a drama company with Christian credentials makes plain what is their up-front stance.

Drama, as my co-writer has shown, has been part and parcel of human expression, and at certain times in Christian history central to its telling the story. However in recent times, owing to the advent of major theatre productions focussing on Jesus, there has been considerable activity. In some instances this has been deliberate, for there has been a conscious attempt to counteract the seemingly alien forces of a secular land. Such plays have dared to tell people what the faith and Jesus are really about.

The success of musicals such as *Hair*, *Superstar* and *Godspell* created a sense of unease in some sections of the Christian world. Whilst many churches took their parishioners in hired coaches into London's West End for an evening out or an assumed spiritual kick, others decided they would try to counteract the pernicious influence of what they saw as suspect productions. They promised the world the true Jesus. They would confront those musicals that had enjoyed such triumph in the London West End and New York's Broadway. They would present the true Jesus.

So, it was said, at least in many a far-fetched claim. Much of it was patently absurd. It meant they could cast Christians and not actors who simply pretended they were religious. Well, that was the argument or is it hope? However rarely would this Jesus touch his vital Jewish self. He would be a product of Western understanding.

And there came forth with a big budget, *Lonesome Stone*. The publicity machine rolled into positive action with a number of engaging sentiments, such as, "First time in a secular theatre – what *Jesus Christ Superstar* and *Godspell* failed to present."

It admitted that *JCS* and *Godspell* had left their impact upon many Christians and naturally the effect was harmful. The writers of *Lonesome Stone* promised a story of what Jesus is doing now, by His Spirit, in thousands of lives. It would be a multi-media production of the Jesus Generation portrayed in music, film, and drama. The essentially American group of predominantly young people felt that Christian productions seldom attain the artistic level of those in the secular theatre, and as a result go unnoticed. *Lonesome Stone* would be different. It wasn't. It was a million miles away.

It did not find a West End slot, instead it occupied one of London's most famous music venues, the art deco Rainbow, in North London. The generosity of the Deo Gloria Trust and the Jesus Family commune from Upper Norwood provided the necessary, and not inconsiderable, finance. With *JCS* and *Godspell* still on the radar screens of media personnel it was not too difficult to interest those in the media both religious and secular.

Although the web site indulges in satisfaction and seems to suggest it was a success, there were few kind words from either religious or secular press. It was for the most part an astonishing piece of amateur work that would sit uneasily with the best 'amateur' productions, of which there are many. London like New York is a theatre city and for anyone who presents theatre there is a fairly knowledgeable clientele. They did not like it. It has to be asked whether the commune really knew theatre. Its poster image of Jesus was the bearded and long-haired Jesus, the sort of guy I would meet on the Berkeley campus in the summer of '69.

Possibly in the right context and place, *Lonesome Stone* could have made some kind of impact, certainly away from critics, general theatre-goers, and more so a large theatre space. However, it was beset by a deep desire of many to tell the Jesus story, and perhaps this motive with its accompanying enthusiasm and false dreams, led them to imagine they knew more about theatre craft than they obviously did.

Christians of the time brought other musicals into the arena and not all explored in any sense the person of Jesus. America exported across the Atlantic the religious musicals *Come Together*, *The Witness* and *If My People*. It was astonishingly suggested that *Come Together* might be *Messiah* of the 20ᵗʰ century.

Church people who appreciated these works perhaps did so because they felt comforted rather than disturbed. *Buzz Magazine*, the Christian monthly for a predominantly young readership, said it was all about hugging and shouting 'hallelujah'. It was claimed that *Come Together* would change the nation, which in reality seems no more plausible than saying a tribe of three-legged women has been discovered in the mountains of Wales. These were popular presentations. They did draw large crowds. The figures were quite astounding in many places. Some found new faith, others felt revitalised, voices spoke of a new movement of the Spirit and many gained a sense of righteousness over the heathen who need to be saved.

In Kent, at St. Nicholas' Church, Sevenoaks, and among the young people known collectively as "Contact" there was a production, *I AM*. It was borne out of a series of productions of *Come Together* that had been put on between January and Easter, 1975. The production had three parts, each expressing the nature of God; God the Father and Creator; God the Son; God the Holy Spirit. The style of each section varied significantly.

There was folk music, a bit of Handel, a bit of Bach and some self-composition in *Alive*, a folkish musical that originated through the famous St. Martins-in-the-Field, and inspired by its curate of the 1970s, Hugh Maddox. It was not without its interesting moments. Maddox told me, "A couple of drunks interrupted and sort of got killed with Jesus at the crucifixion. They went down with the crowd that mobbed him!" For Maddox there was something special about presenting it in this famous location. During performances ambulances could be heard arriving at nearby Charing Cross Hospital. Police and fire services and life's human wanderers, and a collection of free loaders from the meths-drinkers to the junkies, displaced and homeless walked in. In this instance many of the audience had no church connection, they merely happened to be passing.

Here, as with a later musical yet to be mentioned *A Man Dies*, there was a general sense that anything can happen and in the midst of the turmoil of the play and outside interruptions walked the Christ for all people; someone accepting the meths-drinkers, the college student, the fashionable visitor. Not far away from St Martin's there was *JCS* and *Godspell*.

Maddox felt *Alive* was more 'real', even if the dancing at times was almost banal, but "sincerity and freshness" shone through. So too *Alive* threw into the ring a Jesus who kept asking people what they were doing and why they ignored God's reality.

A group of believers in the Oxford area, Cuddington Gospel Outreach, hired the 1700-seater Oxford New Theatre for their musical *Yesterday Today Forever,* aka *YTF.* Although they engaged an established professionally RADA trained Nigel Goodwin as director, for the most part it was a willing brave troupe of people hardly ready to take on the New, let alone an audience. Their enthusiasm and determination to take risks deserves some acknowledgement, but the choice of a 1700 seater was not exactly wise either in the need to fill seats or adapt to a large stage space.

Musically it was rock to Elizabethan, "using modern techniques in theatre and music as sensitively and professionally as possible". The text was a musical drama of the life of Christ from Genesis to Revelation, something *JCS* did not do. They shared an empathy with *Come Together*, and so would say, "We believe the end result will be the same – glorifying God." Naturally this, and some later attempts to emulate *JCS*, came with an album, and in this instance the blurb declared, "it is without question the most ambitious and stunning Christian musical ever to be produced in Britain."

People are welcome to think this.

A Swedish group, *Choralerna*, bobbed along with *Living Water* using material based on St. John's Gospel. A talented outfit, Reflection, who were very much into moving the Christian Church into new areas of liturgy in worship, delivered *Hosanna!* and *Sonburst*. However well done, these works were not likely to make much impression in popular culture.

During this fertile period of the 1970s the most likely 'class act' and possible future epic came from Adrian Snell, classically trained at the Leeds College of Music. His fifth project *The Passion* promised much. A concept work, something of a rock opera, recorded with the Royal Philharmonic Orchestra, the London Welsh Male Voice Choir and the English Chamber Singers. Each major biblical character was taken by different vocal leads with Adrian Snell singing the role of Jesus.

It began with the song 'Gethsemane'. Snell said at the time that the song came from his longing to attempt the simple expression of what must have been the most intense mental and spiritual moments in the life of Jesus, the anticipation of the Cross, the utter loneliness of rejection alongside the knowledge that this was the fulfilment of his mission.

Snell was 15 when he wrote the song and the sentiments had stayed with him. So it gathered pace, one song a year! The material appeared in a low-budget album entitled *Fireflake*. Snell still hungered for better and bigger things and the time came when he could rethink and rework the existing material, write new material and make the album a complete concept. Snell said in an interview at the time, "it gives me the opportunity to present the crucifixion in a way that should communicate to as wide and varied a public as did *Superstar* and *Godspell*." *The Passion* toured 24 cities in the UK and parts of Europe.

However, there were several negative factors to such a hope. Although Snell wrote some of his material before the two musicals he was nonetheless drawing on their success. Secondly, his known market was a mix of ages within the

Christian church. He did not merge into the Jesus youth culture that was largely rock-orientated. He had no standing in that world and his songs, while evocative and beautiful, were not ones to be picked up by a major record company with tentacles into radio stations and the pop press. Here of course we return to the magical marketing of *Superstar* that could engage some of the best rock singers and musicians; people who commanded major respect, although some of their fans might have wondered why they would be involved in some kind of religious project.

The Salvation Army, particularly in the persons of John Gowans and John Larsson, were well to the fore during the Seventies with *Jesus Folk* (1972) *Spirit* (1975), *Glory* (1977), *Blood of the Lamb* (1979) and much later *The Son of Man* (1988). These were 'witness' pieces rather than works exploring character and situation, offering little for the actor. This is not to say that, within their audience boundary, the pieces were not received enthusiastically. They also have to be seen as introducing a considerable degree of difference to that great Christian body; whereas in the general theatre world they would find it hard to raise an eyebrow. *Rock* was the work of David Winter, Peter Bye and Roger Hurrell. Winter had been influential in the Christian journey of Cliff Richard, edited *Crusade* and would become at a later date the head of religious radio programmes at the BBC. Bye worked in the record industry and over the years, has exercised considerable presence in the more professional arena of Christian expression that preserves sanity. Hurrell wrote and sang songs and he too remains a positive influence. *Rock* focussed on Peter's self-understanding and of course relationship with Jesus. Its songs appeared on an album issued by Marshall, Morgan & Scott. Bye was involved with the English translation of a German drama, *John,* and here the late Roy Castle took the main role. On both *John* and *Rock,* Bye used the talents of session singers.

The 1980s brought Robert Rigby's *Rockstar*, a title that seemed somewhat dated, in view of being almost a complete decade on from *JCS*. Hadn't we all become smitten or immune to a pop-sounding Jesus and Gospel? It wasn't without its supporters, especially Paul Davis, then Editor of the monthly *New Christian Music*.

Also making considerable media waves, partly due to the amount of money thrown its way, came *Alpha and Omega,* a musical based on the last book in the Bible, that of *Revelation*. Its world premiere was at Coventry Cathedral. The Young Musicians' Symphony and opera singers from Glyndebourne's Festival took part. While it made for an interesting evening the musical lacked real focus and if Revelation represents the ultimate coming together of all things in Christ then that was not apparent. It was more of a general cry for peace.

Revving up at this time, and to continue almost to his sad passing at a very early age of 57, on November 11, 2007, Methodist minister and evangelist Rob Frost had an especial focus on dramatic production. His plays were mostly performed in theatres which were hired for days or a week or more. His casts were built around some professional actors and fleshed out by amateurs. In towns and cities where a visit was scheduled amateur actors would rehearse ahead and then meet up with the cast for production rehearsal. The shows had a variable quality, and the process was not helped in dramatic terms by Rob delivering a fiery Gospel message at the end of a production. Obviously in the context of his mission work he would not agree. Others would at the very least say any production should be able to stand on its own two feet, if it does not, then it must be jettisoned.

Much of the musical input in his productions came from a talented musician and arranger Paul Field, who had once sung with the group Nutshell and which would became the 'new' Nutshell. By 1983 they were Network 3. He found his songs covered by known artists including Cliff Richard, Barry McGuire and Sheila Walsh. While I'm sure Rob Frost would have hoped that his presentations would draw in the un-churched they were mainly enthusiastically attended by Methodist people and droves of young people who once gave that Church some of its zip. In some Methodist areas there was an almost three-line whip to ensure the theatres were packed, not least because the financial strain was near to breaking point on several occasions.

The musical *Hopes and Dreams* spawned a British national number one pop hit in a separate form from the show's version. The million selling hit of 'The Millenium Prayer' was recorded by Britain's superstar Cliff Richard. Musically, it was Paul Field's arrangement of 'Auld Lang Syne' and which was tailored to fit the words of The Lord's Prayer. The show itself took songs and dance, provoking and amusing sketches that came out of exploring the many facets of the Lord's Prayer. Material here, as with other Frost dramatic works, was penned by Stephen Deal. Its ending attracted much attention with the cast in gold finery as they enacted what some called a heavenly hoedown.

Frost saw Jesus in a fairly conservative evangelical framework, as someone who saves, who steers us away from the gates of hell, who promises new life to those who wish to be born again. I have talked many a time with Rob Frost, and he names a speech of mine at the NIE event in Nottingham in the 1990s as instrumental in setting him out on his ministry. He certainly loved drama but in view of where he was he saw it as a mission tool. Frost established within Methodism, but open to all, the very successful Easter People. Drama was very much part of what was offered at an event that lasted almost a week and was given time in late-night fringe and cabaret, as at Spring Harvest,

Frost made his dramatic foray within a denomination that had always encouraged drama, and was famed for general dramatic presentations, not least the often stunning annual event for the Methodist Association of Youth Clubs at the Royal Albert Hall, in London. Outside of that, Methodism had encouraged drama through its Creative Arts Department, not least through the efforts of Rachel Newton who was at one time Secretary of the Drama Committee of the Methodist Church, and Sara Duckworth. Sadly, Methodism in one of its ever growing moments of self-mutilation has largely dismantled this area and a paid post is no longer operative. That is not say that drama doesn't take place, for the pages of *The Methodist Recorder* frequently report on churches 'putting on' plays.

In several other books I have singled out the production of *A Man Dies* as 'the' finest piece of basically amateur work although it was professionally directed by Ewan Hooper with text from a young clergyman with an ear for words and rhyme, Ernest Marvin. Hooper would become the first director of the Scottish National Theatre.

I have unreservedly recommended it as something deeply moving, in part because the director and writer allowed it to breathe. It is notoriously difficult to let a piece develop and live when all the time a sub-text is forever pressing its claim.

The sub-text is in the motive for doing a piece. A number of questions must be asked, such as, "Is the piece worthy in itself? Irrespective of all other factors is it worth presenting?" The difficulty for some Christians when it comes to drama is that they either do not understand the discipline or they wish first and foremost to say something; so they find/develop a play, claiming their work is inspired by the very breath of God. So it all goes ahead.

When I see a bad 'religious' piece of drama it may be because someone has kept interfering from the word go. This thinking may contain such sentiments as to whether what is done and said may offend, whether it does preach Christ openly, whether it will herald a new spirit in the church or bring young people in, whether it will pacify those who think drama is not for the church, whether people will fill in a decision or visitation card. These may not be consciously expressed – they will hover. People feel it. The actor will be tense. The director should simply clear his or her rehearsal space of all this.

The actors in *A Man Dies* were from the Locklease Estate in Bristol. It was a piece that came out of a situation, the not unfamiliar one of how to translate the Faith into something that can be understood by teenagers who already had their own culture with its rituals. It was not an imposed piece and thus not one where older people float what they think young people should accept and believe.

The play had a rawness, an artistic honesty. It certainly stated Christian faith, but it did so without baggage. It talked of Jesus within teen culture and youth aspirations. You believed the characters. You felt they were not uncomfortable with the text. They related to each other.

A Man Dies has disciples puzzled by events, something *Superstar* in another decade would have us accept. Yet Marvin in his text would introduce into the equation their basic trust and confidence, irrespective of the puzzling.

> We weren't sure we could do what he said
> We felt like children away from home
> Till we trusted his power
> and remembered his words
> And we didn't have to go it alone

The musical went through various incarnations before it ended up at the Royal Albert Hall, London, and the Colston Hall, Bristol, and eventually to the nation's television screens. It was product of the late 1950s and the early 1960s, and all the more remarkable for that. In its time it managed to have questions asked in the Houses of Parliament over its perceived obscenities. While Mary Magdalene in *Superstar* would refer to Jesus' humanity in "He's a man, he's just a man" *A Man Dies* a decade of years earlier had Mary rather fancying Jesus. The idea that a women or even women might have a crush on bachelor Jesus was too much for some, and an attempt was made to either have the thought (in a look and glance) and lines and song removed or that the whole production should cease.

Such were the times, but even with the right press behind it, it could still be an uncomfortable journey for a production. Should Jesus have found a man the outcry would have been louder. One can only assume that Jesus had no interest or even a thought for woman or man. As a previous chapter has shown, not all have been willing to settle for this 'hands off' stance.

Jesus, in *A Man Dies,* would doubtless gain the current description of 'cool' for he was unfazed, lacking in pomposity, simply around and gaining strength through presence. Jesus and the disciples were costumed in blue jeans, doubtless these days the programme notes would have added the sponsorship of a jeans company. The seeming lack of sartorial elegance drew a critical response.

One letter writer commented: "I call it scandalous to put our Saviour and his disciples in such dress. Would those who see learn anything from it, anything holy from such a play?"

Another saw it as mockery and desecration. Another writer decried the length of hair of male actors, in itself an odd statement since if jeans were not worn in first century times, long hair was certainly the norm. In the end the plea to the Marvin-Hooper duo was for them to introduce their young people to the matchless English of Cramner in the *Book of Common Prayer*.

While *Superstar* attracted howls of anguish from certain quarters because it employed the rock genre, *A Man Dies* was more precarious back in the days of the three chord guitarist, or a music scene embellished by *The Shadows*. One critic saw the subjugation of the Church to rock 'n' roll, as if *A Man Dies* represented the endless variations of world Christendom.

Virulent criticism was tempered by approval comment. The esteemed musician and commentator Erik Routley said it was a remarkable adventure in pop language. He saw the whole presentation showing how the very 'brutality' of the pop style can contribute something to Christian drama and that pop dancing can say something in a church setting. *A Man Dies* was contrasted with Bernstein's *Chichester Psalms*, for while the former had a simple fluidity and ease, the latter required too much production, too much orchestral and choral apparatus to be liturgical.

The basic theatre structure of *A Man Dies* revolved around the use of an upper stage and the main floor. The great moments of ministry of Jesus are acted out on the upper stage, while a crowd of youngsters occupy the main floor. From time to time the latter become part of the play and the person of Jesus passes through.

Little is spoken – much is in the world of mime and dance. There are brief passages of the Bible and numerous songs. Routley astutely observed that we had the other side of dance, not as a set piece of performance but being seen almost as natural as walking or running. "The careless, terrified dance of life which proceeds with complete neglect of what the Redeemer is doing. The ground-bass, as it were is provided by a Gospel narrative in song which appears in sections as the mime proceeds." *A Man Dies* should have taught many an aspiring drama troupe that theatre is not necessarily about words, that they are merely one element (and overdone) for there is silence, symbol, action, a gesture, and so forth.

There were several attempts to stage this. One of the most successful came from the Mill Hill Council of Churches, London. It was directed by Rex Walford, a lecturer at the then Maria Grey College of Education. He saw *A Man Dies* as a complete acceptance of teenage culture without someone editing out aspects that were not congenial. He saw the production translating biblical narrative into some kind of reality. There was an important and interesting element that stands as a lesson to anyone who takes a piece based on a particular culture, even if for both parties the view of Christ is found acceptable.

A Man Dies emanated from a basically working-class area. Mill Hill had its low-income streets, especially as it sprawled toward Burnt Oak, but basically it was a fairly typical middle-class London suburb. There was a degree of wealth visible. While teenage culture at any one time has similarities he was well aware that different social strata groupings do produce differences, He was also concerned to adapt it slightly so that it would appeal outside of the teenage syndrome. Hindsight says he succeeded but at the time it seemed an uncertain move.

As with the original, he recruited an excellent beat group, he kept around fifty per-cent of the songs and incorporated some well-known spirituals. He also brought into play several numbers from the then popular West End show, *Black Nativity*. The satire and humour of the original was sharpened and he added several revue style items. Walford was a brilliant director and from here he went on to produce a stirring version of my own favourite musical *West Side Story*. One thing seems plain from this, you have to have a brilliant director – that sounds slightly crass, I feel, to some people; I have in mind those who hear me bewailing another financial pre-production crisis and simply say "why do you need a director?" A brilliant director, as a brilliant choir conductor can take an average group of people with limited expectancies and take them to a higher plane.

Devoid of something to protest against it's interesting that in more recent times many of the texts stemming from the Christian community do not focus on Jesus. Rather they choose material based on Old Testament literature such as Esther, Ruth, David and Moses. There almost seems a fear of presenting aspects of Jesus' ministry. In the case of some of these productions there has been urgent mailing for Christians to support these works and presumably impress the secular powers, so that transfer and money underpinning might see one or more works reach Shaftsbury Avenue, London's most visible theatre street.

Doubtless many churches with their youth groups have attempted to emulate *A Man Dies*, and certainly over the years I have been sent many scripts, including among them *First Rock* which was presented by the Shrewsbury Methodist Circuit Young People in 1985. The original performances had 10 singers, piano, keyboard, thee guitars and bass, with the music arranged accordingly. As with other productions it followed closely the Gospel narratives. So, in terms of Jesus, in the particular section that was headed 'Caesarea Philippi' we have Jesus asking "Who do people say I am?" The answer is found in the Gospel passage. There is some sense of pulling back the Scripture layers but Jesus says the recorded words, as given in the appropriate translation that is used. The most interesting area came with the songs where the writers obviously felt freer to go their own way, although careful to work within the known framework. Hence a verse such as:

> Dig right down to the start of it all
> A man named Simon who heeded the call
> Jesus needed someone before he could build
> Foundation stone of a whole new world.

Unlike those of *A Man Dies*, the text and songs in *First Rock* do not draw either inspiration or reference from teen culture, or the machinations of culture in general. In this it runs with much else that has been produced on Jesus from the church area. That is not to say that the piece did not make an impact upon those who took part, or those who attended the production. It does though make *A Man Dies* an extraordinary piece for its time, with its depth and vision, its willingness to see Jesus and the Gospel narratives within the risky venture of transitory youth culture, although of course the overall needs of the young are fairly constant: which in part might be seen as to love and be loved, to find some security, self-respect and – hopefully – creative avenues.

Not unexpectedly there have been numerous attempts in this multi-media time to find ways of engaging young people in Christian concepts and teaching, with drama one of the main tools.

An interesting book by Michael E. Moynahan, *Once Upon a Mystery* sub-titled *Gospel Mini-dramas for Churches and Schools*, appears for all its often illuminating thoughts, to suffocate possibilities. Rather than inviting exploration and a non-prescriptive approach, the book seems to reveal instead a desire to lead its readers to confine their questions to what the author considers to be accepted Christian doctrine. Hence, for example, when young actors are preparing to play Jesus, they are invited to consider such concepts as:

In what ways is Christ:	»	a Lawgiver?
» » » » »	»	the Mercy of God?
» » » » »	»	the Judgement of God?
» » » » »	»	a Redeemer?
» » » » »	»	the Word-Made-Flesh?

There are a further eleven questions with their suggested descriptions. The writer asks the young person to suggest other images of Christ, to say which images or pictures of Christ mean least, which are most comforting and those that are the most challenging. It is highly likely that the actor would either feel drawn to say something that fits the given titles or be totally nonplussed! Such titles may well have come from much discussion and reflection within the historic Christian community, and so assume almost a 'sacred' no-touch, but they have little direct meaning to an actor's intentions. If an actor is given the role of Jesus how can he come to terms with any of those descriptions?

In Scene Four of the section of the book dealing with Jesus Christ, a number of people give their views on Jesus, with a narrator saying, "Let's hear what people of his day had to say about who he was."

There follows a list of players by number, although names are given to the numbers at the commencement of the material.

"And he did it on the Sabbath. He was a lawbreaker!"

"I was dead and he brought me back to life."

"Only God is the Lord of life. He had a Messianic complex!"

"He was a blasphemer! Only God can forgive sins!"

At the conclusion all the players freeze, and the narrator comes down to the acting area and says: "So there were and continue to be differences of opinion. Please tune in next week for another edition of the show that asks that haunting question: 'Who do you say they are?' Until next time, this is your host. Garth Ashbeck, saying: Who do you say you are?"

It is, in fact, unlikely that any actor would identify with the views expressed or be led to examine their own identity through this activity. Indeed these are views found in the Gospel narratives but are in themselves unhelpful if they come, as it were, out of context.

Many of the reflective questions and exercises prove extremely useful from a biblical group study perspective; for instance material that falls under the heading 'To Rule The World With Justice,' but while giving the actor some kind of background and stimulus from a faith perspective the actual dialogues springing from the chosen New Testament passage leave few choices. It would seem a subject is chosen. The next stage is listing a number of thoughts and expressions, some safe to the chosen view, and a few less so. These are then put in the mouths of chosen characters. Next comes the spoken stage to be followed by a discussion as to what 'such and such' should have said or not said, and whether the view has a rightness from a pre-determined Christian position. A not dissimilar tenor - albeit markedly given three paragraphs – can be found in Issue 46 of the British publication *Roots*. This lively journal says it provides "worship and learning for the whole church." It offers material for the Sunday gathering ranging from reflection on the biblical passage of the day, to a mini-sermon for the lazy suggested prayers, hymn selections and ideas for what has become

known as 'all-age worship.' The text often suggests improvised drama, and in the case of Issue 46 for March 14, 2010,
the focus is on the third of the stories in the well-known and
popular fifteenth chapter of St. Luke's Gospel. The worship
leader is bidden to ask whether anyone in the gathering
would like to act out the story. Anyone well practiced in the
art of general audience involvement will know that such a
suggestion can be the kiss of death. Perhaps though the
writer has in mind a stand-by crew! Four people are needed
to portray the younger son, Father, elder son and servant.
The worship leader, in the role of Jesus tells the story. What
next? "You can either give each character a script or let them
repeat their words after you." In the second paragraph the
writer in pragmatic fashion deals with the horror of there
not being enough microphones. The solution rests in one
person reading while the four 'actors' simply mime appropriately. Even this latter suggestion produces a shudder to
the system, for the whole 'thought-form' lying behind a set
of seemingly easy ideas is distressing. Story-telling and
mime are notoriously difficult, or, at very least, demand
many hours of work if a text is to come alive. Improvised
work is equally hard. For instance, those who write and
perform the various works under the name of Applecart
spend many hours, even days in devising and rehearsal, and
their brilliant storyteller is a trained actor. That is not to
suggest that only professionals should be allowed near
anything that might appear to be drama, but anyone writing
and suggesting such a process should be indicating that this
week's work will take a dedicated three to six hours work,
and even that is a fairly loose framework unless directed by a
skilled person rather than simply by a do-gooder.

I have instanced these texts in some detail because they
follow a similar pattern and contain approaches that are
largely anathema to some of the concepts brought forward
in this book. There is nothing intrinsically wrong with the
suggested approach, it is the chosen way of many, and,
unfortunately, it is given the description of 'drama'. Indeed,
within the often tiresome process of conventional worship
such 'drama' may bring something akin to interest.

Significantly the comments from various people on the back cover of the first book suggest that for many it contains the possibility of good times in making clear Christian truths. Such beliefs are also endemic in many general church drama scripts. The continual assumption made, especially when scriptural words are given a modern gloss, rests in assuming that words mean something in themselves, without consideration as to what might be the connection. The brilliant, and often ignored, facet of the Gospel writing rests in knowing the target. In our way of dealing with Scripture, especially the new, we isolate different passages, wrench them out of context and so find no through line. It should be remembered that at one time there were no chapters and no verses, it simply flowed.

The nearest example I can find to illustrate this is Pasolini's, film *Gospel of Matthew*, while in Britain various actors such as Paul Alexander and Lance Pierson have among their own highly skilled repertoire straight readings of a Gospel narrative. Their difficulty rests in persuading people to 'stay with it' and so at some time realise just what it is all about! Church lectionaries for preachers attempt to present a co-ordinated flow of material but I have never heard an officiant relate the Gospel of the day to the previous week or weeks, other than in Advent or approaching Easter.

While the 1970s and 1980s spanned quite a few productions, since then the cupboard had been relatively bare although there have been countless school and church presentations of *Joseph, JCS* and *Godspell*. In the main, churches look for works with considerable casts. They want to involve as many as possible as that means less financial worries, for a cast of 50 can generate family following in addition to any church member support. Christmas and Easter bring forth a plethora of dramatic texts.

As with some productions I have specifically mentioned, many of those I have read merely fit existing Scriptural words into the mouths of the participants, and while providing some would say another way of hearing Scripture read, it is a moot point whether these moments offer anything more. On occasions the motive is more about involving people and encouraging some to attend church by giving them something to do rather than any respect for the words used.

However some of the creative slack may be occasioned by the growth of professional and semi-professional based Christian originated companies, although some such as my own Jasperian Theatre Company would prefer to be considered a theatre company predominantly presenting religious based material. We would stress that whatever we perform must have the discipline of the theatrical and dramatic form at the forefront. JTC only utilises ex-drama school actors, and in most cases has demanded Equity membership. Many of the actors have West End and other major theatre credits.

JTC asks for an empathy for the material we present and yes, for the part most actors do have some form of Christian allegiance that in religious expression can cover a wide area. JTC has explored many a famous life, such as the Booths; John and brother Charles Wesley; Evan Roberts, the young man at the forefront of the Welsh Revival of 1904-6; Billy Bray, the extraordinary Cornishman of faith and more general themes. The texts have stressed how contemporary many of the issues of their time remain, whether personal or social. Catherine Booth was railing against the City and the bankers in the 19th century! It needs to be emphasised that JTC is centrally concerned with how each of these people and others saw Christ and how it affected what they did. The 2010 production for Lent and Easter, *Friday Friday Sunday Sunday* focussed on the nature of forgiveness and acceptance. No one played Jesus – it was set in a contemporary context - but its text stressed very much the Jesus who frees people from areas that inhibit or deny both personal and community growth.

In British terms, these companies can mean the Riding Lights Company, Rhema, Saltmine, the Covenanters and Palaver; and these are singled out because they pay their actors. Some Christian based companies employ younger actors with a Christian conviction but may pay poorly.

In some cases, as Rhema, The Covenanters and Saltmine, actors are hired on a year or more contracts and their work has a much more distinctly evangelistic edge and extends into other areas such as workshops and testimony, and very much into schools. JTC casts in the manner of any theatre company and Riding Lights casts for its productions.

Companies such as Riding Lights, Rhema and Saltmine, unlike say JTC, employ staff. Saltmine's annual revenue exceeds a million pounds. These companies have a more direct evangelistic attack. Rhema has worked mostly in schools and the drama is tailored towards presentation that makes young people aware of Gospel claims. In 2010 the company presented *Easter Tales*. Rhema's manager Mark Wade bubbles with enthusiasm for the variety of approaches their presentations make. The Arts Centre Group membership listing at the beginning of the last decade of the 20th century also named Resurrection Theatre Company, Jakes Ladder Company, Footprints Theatre Trust, Seeds and Elle M Theatre Company.

New companies spring up from time to time, one of which is Minimum Theatre, an ecumenical drama group, and based at Sage Cross Church, Melton Mowbray. In 2006 it had a mini-tour performing a new play *Consequences*, written by their director and Methodist local preacher Richard Adams. The group formed in 2003 specialises in updating biblical material.

Riding Lights has had more influence than any other. It originated as a community theatre project in York in 1977. Its roots are in street theatre for CSSM missions and aiding the ministry of David Watson at St Michael-le-Belfry. The co-founder Paul Burbridge with Murray Watts, recalls how the Bible, *Beano* and *Beyond the Fringe* were all feeding into their background of a creative Evangelical tradition. Burbridge speaking to Pat Ashworth of the *Church Times* (28 March 2008) said, "If there's an appropriate theatrical vehicle for the Christian message as a whole, it has to be comedy, not tragedy. It can't end with Good Friday, but must go through to Easter."

Under its umbrella there can be three diverse companies simultaneously performing throughout the UK and abroad. It has been acclaimed for mainstream productions of classic plays and stage adaptations of chosen literature. In the great tradition established centuries ago with the medieval

Mystery Plays, a broad Christian perspective underpins its work. Its artist director, Paul Burbridge, talks of the company staging high quality productions, to reach a broad audience with work of lasting value, to awaken a strong dramatic tradition within the Christian community.

However long before JTC, Riding Lights, and most others first breathed life, there existed Theatre Roundabout and Aldersgate Productions. The latter company was formed in the wake of *Godspell* and *Superstar*.

Aldersgate Productions for many years had its own base Westminster Theatre, London although technically it had to hire the premises just like any other group. Its aim was to present material that was no more out of place in professional terms than anything found in mainstream theatres in the Victoria area of London, although its seating capacity at around four hundred, was somewhat smaller. It had its detractors who were aware that the philosophy of Moral Rearmament was very much to the fore of an overall agenda.

Many of its works were written by Peter Howard and Alan Thornhill and texts dealt with moral and ethical issues of the time. To many in the mainstream church, and particularly Methodists, one of its most successful productions was *Ride! Ride!* written by Alan Thornhill. The production in 1976 was followed by *Sentenced to Life* by Malcolm Muggeridge and Alan Thornhill, followed by *About Face*, a morality play with masks by Steve and Janet Stickley. In 1985 they had a runaway success with *The Lion, The Witch and the Wardrobe*, adapted by Glyn Robbins from the classic children's novel by C.S. Lewis. Later came another classic from C.S. Lewis *Narnia*. Ronald Mann, the secretary told *The Methodist Recorder* in 1986 that he viewed Aldersgate as, "hopefully, a voice of the churches in the theatre and media world."

Theatre Roundabout began presenting Christian theatre in January 1960, touring full-time in 1961 with around 40,000 performances; most were two-person shows featuring Sylvia Read and William Fry. The latter says their policy has been to offer work that is profound enough for the Church and entertaining enough for the theatre. The two retired from full-scale performances in July 2007. Among their two-handed repertoire were *Shadowlands, Canterbury's*

Burning and the *Pilgrim's Progress*. The doyen of reviewers Harold Hobson wrote, "I came out of a sense of duty and stayed for delight."

In 2008 the end came for The Wayfarers drama group that had since its formation in 1965 presented many stimulating works in Yorkshire. Among their repertoire was *Christ in the Concrete City* written by a prolific religious playwright of the time, Philip Turner. The company performed *Redemption* by Gordon Honeycombe and received much praise. The company never charged for entrance, and said their work was part of a church service. They relied on the generosity of the public for funding.

Frank Topping is a professional actor and Methodist minister. He and his wife June have their own production company. From time to time, and with a variety of productions, the one-man show hits the road (she is on lighting). Topping brings professionalism into the Christian arena but much of his experience has been more secular. His early fame for a certain television soap opera constituency lies in his role as the priest who married Ken and Deidre Barlow. For others he is remembered for his partnership with Donald Swann in the London West End production of their show Swann with Topping. Brian Sibley a prominent member of the Christian-based, Arts Centre Group, and a radio playwright of some distinction was very much involved in new scripting. Topping has had many books of prayers and thoughts published and for many years he regularly appeared on the Terry Wogan morning radio show on BBC Radio2.

In terms of sheer numbers attending, few could disagree that the most successful stage output belongs to Christian Music Ministries, Roger Jones and family. The Jones catalogue is extensive. His forte lies in an ability to score music that is tuneful, catchy, and within reach of the keen singer. Wherever his productions go, previous to his arrival a choir has been established. One of the doyens of the 'praise' world Chris Bowater sees his music establishing a repertoire right across the spectrum of the church, serving as a bridge between traditional roots and the growing renewal churches. For Jones his work is about bringing people into a living relationship with God and Jesus. His work does not debate or question, or throw open to question the Faith. Originally a school teacher in the 1960s and '70s he began writing songs for his school choir before deciding on a full-time Christian music ministry. Central to the Pentecost, Churches Together event, Cumbria 2010 was *Wildfire*. The musical play begins with Pentecost and the transforming effect the Spirit had on Stephen and his family. It moves on to recall the signs and wonders that were performed, Saul's persecution of early believers, how the widows and orphans were cared for, and ultimately to Stephen's martyrdom. Following Paul's conversion he returns to Stephen's family and acknowledges that Stephen's faith was an example of God's love for all.The latter interpolation does leave the question of how far a writer can add to Scripture without people assuming it is in the very Word itself.

In 2009, two Methodists who are also well proven actors, Perer Moreton and a now Methodist minister in the Tower Hamlets circuit of London, Phil Summers, began what they called Applecart in an East London public house on a Sunday Evening. Summers displayed his story telling ability while Moreton engaged in dramatic sketches, general commentary, and displayed his song writing ability with largely blues style numbers.

Inevitably in this brief survey there will be people who will feel somewhat deflated that their names are missing. In the small-time theatre business recognition is far from easy and thanks not exactly plentiful, even from Church circles. You are very much on your own. Within my immediate perspective I single out a few – such as Robin Meredith's New Directions that provides rehearsed play readings of new material, and in itself this is an undervalued aspect of theatre. He, and especially his talented actress wife Christine, have presented many forceful productions throughout Britain. June Boyce Tillman has particular interest in children's music and completed a PhD at the Institute of Education, London, and already possessed a degree in music from St Hughes College, Oxford. She has a number of one-woman performances with particular focus on medieval women mystics. Jesus and the Scriptures come alive in the work presented by actors such as Lance Pierson; Rupert Thompson; the late and incredibly talented Rob Lacey; Anita Palmer; Andrew Graystone; Paul Heyman.

For sheer assault on the human personality, in the mistaken name of Jesus, I know of no British company that can hold a torch to one example of American aggression. Reality Outreach say that their goal and commitment is to form a unified team of committed believers to win the lost back to Jesus Christ. They push forward on the internet their drama *Heaven's Gates & Hell's Flames* and have done so in venues seating fewer than a hundred as well as in the Royal Albert Hall. They claim to have performed to nearly five thousand people. They call their production high impact drama designed "to make people aware of Jesus Christ, Heaven, & Hell and Eternity according to the Bible." Cast and stage crew is kept to a minimum of 35 and a maximum of 50 with the cast speaking 24 parts.

The Times Magazine has reported on the new morality plays that have become the darling of the far right evangelical Christians in America. They termed it "Welcome to the 'hell house', Texas style. "Now they're giving a 21st century twist to medieval damnation tableaux – drink-drive carnage, rapes, abortion scenes – in a bid to terrify teenagers into their Saviour's embrace." A favourite theme in hell houses is showing homosexuals going to Hell. Every weekend evening Trinity Church in Cedar, Texas orders in the requisite buckets of theatrical blood.

It seems parents, anxious to ensure their daughters remain virginal, drive some distance in order that their offspring experience relevant drama, and in this instance it focusses on bloody abortion. 'The Hell Mouth' was much the most popular and eagerly awaited feature of the Miracle plays. It was generally represented as a square, embattled tower, the entrance to which was by way of a gaping and hideous dragon's head, with glaring eyes, enormous mouth, and moveable jaws lined with long, projecting teeth. As Sidney Clarke-Smith tells us in his book *The Miracle Play in England*, fire and smoke came forth when the jaws were opened and the method for this lay with braziers and bellows hidden away behind and vomited from the mouth and nostrils. Drums were beaten, horns blown, tin cans banged and amid the wild din the devil and his imps leapt in and out of the flaming opening, to drag the wicked characters to limbo, or stir up the unhappy occupants of the infernal regions. It was a stage manager's joy.

At the same time a small group of writers, and producers, have come forward providing good texts, rather than starting with some kind of evangelistic premise and then cobbling some thoughts together under a vague umbrella of drama, even if the intent is ensuring Jesus is centre stage. Names here include Les Ellison, Nick Warburton, Brenda Jackson, Kevin Mandry and John Waddington-Feather. There has also been major input by various people with a theatre background, to include the forementioned Paul Burbridge, Robin Meredith, Nigel Forde, James Roose-Evans, Peter Moreton and the sadly missed Michael Austin and yes, others. There is Murray Watts of Riding Lights association but in his own right he wrote *The Fatherland*. It won the London Weekend Television Plays on Stage competition in 1989. Since 1929 Radius has offered extraordinary support to religious drama, from encouraging and giving advice to writers and their scripts, to churches and productions, conferences, workshops, and publishing a magazine. Two patrons are listed in its general credits, the Archbishop of Canterbury and Dame Judi Dench. The latter began her career appearing in a production of the York Mystery plays, and directed by E. Martin Browne. In the United States similar work is found under the umbrella of Christian Theatre Scripts and its founder Sandy Boikan. A monthly newsletter encourages the raising of overall standards.

In one of Methodism's more imaginative postings Michael Austin was in charge of the Theatre Church at Astley Bridge, Bolton. Beneath the stage lay the usual church adornments that by hydraulics could be brought to the stage surface for Sunday worship. It seems as though this was another of those brave misunderstood ventures, there were those good folk who wanted their church to be 'Church," and that means apart from Sunday the visual furniture dressing and flower displays, an empty building for the rest of the time, and running at crippling cost.

Austin was a wonderful character, genial and friendly, knowledgeable and talented. Furthermore, apart from encouraging many companies and actors, Michael Austin and Peter Moreton, are associated with Palaver Productions. For a while his work reached theatreland, and two of his plays *Temptations* and *Betrayals* were performed at the Studio Theatre of the Bristol Old Vic.

Austin had little truck with sloppy theology eating its way into so-called 'religious' subject scripts. He demanded rigorous theological exploration. As I see it, Austin saw his work as a contemporary blending of what is at the root of the past Mystery Plays. In his article Theology Reflects on the Arts, for the *Methodist Epworth Review*, April 1998, he instances from the Penguin classic, *The English Mystery Plays*, where Peter Hepple sees the plays written "as part of a theological message, and were intended no doubt, to be an act of teaching and worship combined." Austin adds that the mystery plays had a hermeneutic function and an apologetic one. He said he saw Palaver Productions being part of the tradition to explain the basic stories of faith to those with a limited access to the literature of faith, or to the rites of faith. In other words, the Mystery Plays were attempts to make 'present' the faith stories through drama. This was his mission for Palaver.

In the same article Austin tells of a group of women who passed him by as they were leaving the theatre, discussing what they had seen.

"Well," said one of the women eventually breaking the tension, "I'm not really sure what to make of that. I really fancied that Jesus!"

Austin comments: "It is a story to laugh about when sharing theatre anecdotes. But also the comment gave me great satisfaction."

Austin said Palaver Productions enjoyed presenting Bible stories for a generation who do not read their Bibles. "For me the exploration of the stories and translating them into drama for urban women and men at the end of the twentieth century has been a fascinating and demanding process. Yet there has also been great satisfaction in knowing that our work has been spoken within Christian tradition. We make demands upon audiences who may be used to entertainment."

CHAPTER EIGHT

Listening And Seeing
– At Home

Until very recently in the forms of communication offered to humankind any talk of Jesus on stage would mean a dramatic production presented in an ascribed location, whether building or open space. It meant that an audience had a degree of power, and actors vulnerability. Hiding away somewhere is the writer and director, even stage manager. The poor actor in a badly written or directed play is the one who receives unsettling coldness out front.

Some of this is true of conventional theatre, and certainly so the small company where actors may perform only feet away from their audience. In a conventional theatre with heavy lighting the audience is presumed to be present, their murmurs, a kind laugh or two, and a few claps remind the cast of their presence. The paying punters can boo and hiss, or simply, as in some cases fail to return after the interval. Radio and television can be switched off, letters written, but it's not the same. Live you can see an actor sweating, see the fear in their eyes as you deduce either he or she is forgetting their lines or simply that somebody else has even jumped some pages of script. I do remember one young actor whispering to me, "Can we go back?"

With the advent of radio, and then television, two new and very powerful media arrived. And drama changed. You could no longer see real human flesh and blood. No one had made a journey, let alone bought tickets. Within minutes millions of people could hear in their own cultural understanding the same material. Outside of a licence to receive, it was available by the flick of a switch, and a choice of the appropriate receiving band. During the early days in the broadcasting transmissions of religion it was hoped male listeners would wear a hat when hearing the word of God read or explained.

The place of religion, let alone the new stage with which the Jesus story could be told, and particularly its relationship with the BBC is brilliantly described in Kenneth M. Wolfe's massive volume *The Churches and The British Broadcasting Corporation 1922-1956* and well sub-titled, *The Politics of Broadcast Religion* (SCM 1984). Wolfe's most disturbing conclusion in his final chapter 'Concluding Perspective' writes of how "few church leaders regarded broadcasting as the most astonishing invitation of all time to twentieth century Christianity to provide as best it could for the spirituality of a newly emerging technological and pluralist society."

The story is often of interference, of denominational power struggles, of avoiding controversy, and an unwillingness of the church to trust the BBC and its professional staff. This chapter confines itself to several notable moments when Jesus took stage through radio (and television) output.

It must be said that this is a cursory glance, but Wolfe's book that takes us only to 1956 has over 600 pages discussing how faith should be presented on radio and television. However fifty or more years later from Wolfe's mighty tome the subject of broadcast faith remains. The BBC continues to receive mail on this subject, so too does the Methodist Church as instanced in a *Methodist Recorder* (November 12 2009) article telling how they receive emails from Methodists around Britain expressing concern about something they may have seen on the BBC, or asking what the church can do to improve the BBC's general, let alone religious, output. The saddest plea from religious listeners is either for more hymn singing programmes or broadcasting of church services.

However to pose a straight-forward question – name the two most influential popularly known twentieth century religious drama titles. It would surely lead to the instant answer of *Jesus Christ Superstar* and *Godspell*. However in terms of radio arguably the most celebrated radio religious drama piece dealing with Jesus from the

1940s onwards is the Dorothy L. Sayers' epic of 1941, *The Man Born To Be King*. We, of course, are dealing with how Jesus has been perceived and staged, and it is not within the province of this text to cover various religious and theological debates, or even the divine plan as found in other Sayers' texts, such as *The Zeal of Thy House*, even if structured around a liturgical framework.

Here, as elsewhere, it is impossible not to be conscious of the simple fact that any depiction of Jesus, let alone God, even Satan, comes annoyingly flavoured with stern criticism. It is not entirely a stage phenomenon. It can be said of Jesus in film. Sometimes one text straddles both worlds. The play *Green Pastures* caused much distress in 1930, and it would be accused of 'sheer blasphemy' when released as a film in 1936. Two years later a film of Christ's life, *From The Manger to the Cross* was refused a licence.

Obviously it is good to say something about a writer's background influences when known. Dorothy Sayers was inspired by the writings of G.K. Chesterton. She had been moved by his image of Christendom as a heavenly chariot, "thundering through the ages, the dull heresies sprawling and prostrate, the wild truth reeling but erect." *The Church Times* writer Adrian Leak in a lengthy feature marking the 50th anniversary of her death in December 2007 wished to say that she embraced the idea with intellectual passion.

"In this she stood in the classical tradition of Christian spirituality which admits no separation between heart and mind."

Dorothy L. Sayers was a child of her time, in so far as she moved in a tradition that since her time has suffered drastically as secularism has infected society as a whole. Within some areas of the Christian churches, theology has become a non-starter with the consequence that either wet liberalism or dumbed down simplification steals the majority audience. Within either sphere any suggestion as to man's sinful nature is conveniently pushed aside. Little is said about God's good grace. There is no real message of redemption or deliverance, just the urging to do a little better.

There is a strong case for arguing that Dorothy Sayers is the last writer to clearly lay down in a dramatic text the Catholic tradition that is so much part of the mystery play tradition. The Catholic standpoint bounces off the belief that human life and history are a part of God's plan. In the mystery plays, as my co-writer has shown, there is a plan that takes one from Creation to Judgement and the climax and central figure is Jesus and what theology terms the Incarnation.

A British writer E. Martin Browne reminds us that the "cosmic and eternal values implicit in God's plan dominate all the works of writers in the Catholic tradition," even when dealing with unbiblical subjects. Browne lectured in the USA and instances *The Satin Slipper* by Paul Claudel, "where the destinies of a few individuals are set against the panorama of history". He would find this evident in the intimate work of Graham Greene and T.S. Eliot.

The Man Born to be King in its time, received much criticism from what appear now to be stuffy pig-headed individuals. They aligned faith with being quintessentially English; those of such a disposition possessed a somewhat limited vision of what it is to uphold the faith. It was seen by them as the process that would involve their marshalling the appropriate forces against the uncouth and dis-respectful philistines – who just happened to be writers and given in error to dramatise the sacred text. In this area it did not matter if they were of Christian persuasion – they should simply not meddle with sacred things.

Another fact, perhaps sounding strange to people in the 21st century and presented by Dorothy L. Sayers in the intro-duction of her classic work, is the statement on page 18 that "The knowledge which the public has of the New Testament is extensive, but in many respects peculiar." By this she meant people have a disjointed awareness of the text rather than, "a coherent history made up of coherent episodes." It did mean that some people believed their 'bits and pieces' qualified them to pass irrefutable judgement.

The 1946 Gollancz publication of the text contains a foreword by J.W. Welch, Director of Religious Broadcasting at the BBC; apparently one of the more adventurous and far-sighted staff members. He explains how he wrote to

Dorothy Sayers asking whether, "she would write a series of plays on the Life of our Lord for broadcasting on *Children's Hour*." He was prompted to do this due to the success of her nativity play *He That Should Come*. The invitation was accepted, but Ms Sayers said her approval came with three conditions: (i) she must introduce the character of our Lord (2) she must be allowed to use the same kind of realism which she had used in her nativity play (3) the text must be in modern speech.

By December 1941 five plays had been written, and the first, dealing with the Nativity, would be broadcast on the Sunday before Christmas 1941.

Ten days before its broadcast the playwright attended a press conference. It was from this occasion that the storm broke. Even before a broadcast, certain sections of the press had decided there was a tasty story to stir their readers into righteous indignation, along the familiar lines where the complainant has not seen or heard what it is that forms the focus of their ire.

A question was asked in the House of Commons.

The text received a very positive response from all the mainline Christian denominations. The BBC saw this as a valuable support as it faced loud and angry noises, but it did postpone the broadcast of the second play by a fortnight, so that it could gather an even greater sense of approval from Christian people, as well as the figureheads of what were then influential voices in Britain.

Reading words about the furore is to find oneself drawn into almost an unreal world – and it must be remembered that at this time Britain was at war, and yet as the bombs fell, and children were evacuated from cities, industry turning to manufacture for the needs of the conflict, this was considered such a serious matter.

The plays were broadcast at monthly intervals from December 1941 to October 1942, and at much shorter intervals during Lent and Holy Week in 1943.

J.W. Welch also dissertated on what partly underlies any revival of interest in Christian faith. He believed a prime factor lay in a fresh study of the life and teaching of Christ.

Listening And Seeing – At Home

He said the task of the Church in any age is to 'reveal' Christ. However the perennial question rests in how to find the method(s) to awaken interest from the lapsed or non-church goer. In this, he believed Dorothy L. Sayers could offer some sense of an answer. He found her use of realism, modern speech and the introduction of the character of our Lord, the person and life and teaching of Christ to take on a new meaning and relevance.

Certainly there were many letters to support his thesis. People found her work exciting, free from conventional church jargon, and in schools and churches people were taking to their Bibles. Her depicting of Christ was not as someone gentle, kind and charming such as Cinderella, "but a real being who can give them strength and courage to love God and be themselves forming their own opinions from Christ's teachings."

The detractors varied from the sane to the almost certifiable. The latter occasioned immediate attention. One writer thought their broadcasting, "made possible the November victories in Libya and Russia." Another group with dubious sanity thought the fall of Singapore in February 1942 was a sign of the divine displeasure with the series. Ms Sayers was accused of personifying the Godhead, "a blasphemy beyond all the blasphemies of which Ms Sayers was accused." The Lord's day Observance Society put aside their strictures on Sunday and complained that, "A sinful man presuming to impersonate the Sinless One! It detracts from the honour due to the Divine Majesty." Various people organised protest groups. There was dismay that the familiar language of the Authorised Version was replaced, and that play should be the chosen means of evangelism. J.W. Welch comments: "The coverings of antiquity were removed and our Lord, for many of us, was alive as never before."

In presenting Jesus she was concerned that he should be seen very much the human being, the man who walked the byways of first century Palestine. "If he did not use colloquial language, he would be a stained glass window, an unreal figure." Of course it would be the case that a sinful man would be impersonating the Sinless One! "In the present instance a man chosen to impersonate the Eternal Son of

God – attributing to Him some words our Divine Saviour never uttered – is a professional actor. Could anything be more distressful to reverent-minded Christians".

The sheer length of the work with its consistency was unrivalled then, and we may never see its like again. Her sheer brilliance keeps finding expression page after page. Of course she did have the advantage of an audience prepared to come on a long journey not expecting to be the recipients of dumbed down presentation nor did she live in a society of spectacle, where in one analysis people themselves aspire to become images and celebrities. Reality is very much on the back burner. Quite what she would have made of Jesus being labelled Superstar is for wondering!

Equally so, it is interesting to speculate how she would view the late 20th century, and the decade following, in which, apparently, anything goes. However, theatre was undergoing major change, in part from the 'tech' side with stage sets assuming almost an importance of their own. That in itself would have meant fewer words, for from the vantage point of today many of her character speeches are long. Her work continues to fascinate and in 2009 Radius published *The Man Born To Be King* as a study course of her cycle of twelve radio plays. The text was by Rex Walford, who had also directed the first linked stage production of all twelve plays at St. Mark's Church, Newnham, Cambridge, UK.

Dorothy L. Sayers may have enjoyed popularity back in the 1940s but by the 1950s the BBC's Religious Department was getting itchy feet. It wanted more religious drama. It became persuaded that drama was the key to the broadcasting of religion, both to the non-churchgoer and to the unschooled churchgoers. The far seeing and perceptive J. Omerod Greenwood of the department felt that most religious drama would be detected a mile off and with other aspects in mind Greenwood saw there was little hope unless the clergy realized that drama and language were not the inert servants of dogma.

His most quotable statement stands for all time: "Good sermons are written by people who are sure they are right; good plays by people who are not." Alongside this pithy statement must go another thought from more recent time.

In their book *Performing the Sacred, Theology and Theatre in Dialogue* Johnson and Savidge point out that the theology that is found in the text on the page becomes something quite different when the play in performance is brought to life by actors and is received and travelled by an audience.

A drama and scriptwriters conference was set up in 1952. It cannot be said that unanimity was found. Also it has to be borne in mind that the BBC had a drama department that was jealously guarded by its practitioners who could ask with some justification what the religious department knew about radio drama.

About this time, T.S. Eliot was warning about the television 'habit' and what he had seen in America had filled him with foreboding. Even the Archbishop of York, Cyril Garbett thought that television was a dangerous invention. It soon became framed in the question; "what exactly was 'that' place for God in the television service?" It seemed that whatever the BBC and the less restricted independent companies might do once they were up and running (1955) there would be clergy and some lay people on their backs. It was not the place for Jesus centre stage. However, after mind-boggling background scenarios, something did happen and in the mid-1950s television showed *Jesus of Nazareth*. For anyone who likes intrigue, the facile, the splendid all rolled into one, the place to read is from page 503 in Kenneth M. Wolfe's *The Churches and The British Broadcasting Corporation*.

Two programmes have remained constant in schedules *Sunday Half Hour* on BBC Radio 2, although no longer a programme that once toured the churches and so had some style and difference, even in dialect, and *Songs of Praise* that does move about. In another year it will become increasingly difficult for them to find a new location, although coming from a space shuttle or on Mars, and perhaps a broken down snow-afflicted Eurostar might be useful suggestions.

Both programmes in their particular way feature hymns, and in a sense bring Jesus on stage in the singing of religious verse. *Songs of Praise* is more overtly into producing the unusual, more so in terms of location than in hymn and song selection. I trust I am right in saying that I was the first to write a script and be involved in dramatic excerpts on the latter, this being the first of its special programmes on the Americans Moody and Sankey that came from the Victoria Hall, Bolton. The second was given to other writers and managed a goodly number of factual errors.

Quite what Dorothy L. Sayers, and those in the BBC Religious Department of the 1950s would have made of *Jerry Springer – The Opera* is an intriguing prospect, although if the answer is brief and terse it may spring from the very debatable decision of the BBC to broadcast it on radio. It should be said that programmers must be adventurous and invite strong criticism. Whether the Springer Opera was the piece to display this, without pushing all things else down the list, is 'the' question. As mentioned earlier an unprecedented 55,000 letters of complaint were sent to the BBC. To a degree any reaction might be one of 'so what?' and to suggest positive strains to the effect that it obviously stirred and moved people, and presumably there were 55,000 or more who did not complain and are not active letter writers to broadcasting corporations. There were some searing letters of support for the BBC's action, not least from the former head of religious broadcasting, and BBC Controller in Northern Ireland, Colin Morris, who thought, among other things, that after 2,000 years Christianity can survive a barrage of swear words.

In the beginning of Morris' article for *The Guardian*, the figure of 63,000 is given. Morris said the governors' Programme Complaints Committee, "was concerned to decide whether the decision to broadcast was in breach of relevant editorial standards, codes and guidelines. But the theological arguments are equally compelling." Morris zeroed in on the person of Jesus. He noted the Jesus of Nazareth whom artists treat like any other historical figure. He thought some Christians might be offended but, "they can't have it both ways by claiming Jesus was a real man, while expecting society to treat him with kid gloves." He instanced the Radio 3 producer Antony Pitts who resigned in protest, "Jesus is my friend."

Morris in common with another commentator on the Springer affair, actor/director Peter Moreton, pointed out that in reality the text was a vicious satire on some aspects of the American way of life, and where Jesus is often merely a commercialised figure in some dubious religious output masquerading as Christian.

In its issue of March 6, 2009, the *Church Times* celebrated with some style the 80th anniversary of the passing from this life of Geoffrey Studdert Kennedy, better known as Woodbine Willie, and especially regarded with great affection by thousands of British servicemen in and after the First World War. Kennedy was an army chaplain who had an extraordinary capacity to get alongside the men who fought in the most difficult circumstances.

His nickname came from his habit of giving the men cigarettes. In his time the *Woodbine* brand vied for the best selling brand with *Players*. He was appalled by the war and on Armistice Day in 1921 he used the word 'madness' to describe its deliberations. It meant he dedicated himself through the political turmoil of the 1920s to making sense of this human tragedy. Several plays have been written that dramatise his obsession with peace and at the same time show how he was well received when he talked war during the conflict – he wanted to see it quickly ended – and how talk of peace produced the alternative reaction. Many Brits in the 1920 wanted revenge and were certainly not in the mood to make any kind of goodwill gesture to the German government.

Sadly Kennedy died at the young age of 45 and his obituary covered a whole page in the *Church Times*, March 15, 1929; in itself a remarkable event since obituaries of such length usually attend the world famous or those of the higher echelons of the Church. Along with Tubby Clayton, the founder of Toc H, Dick Sheppard the loved pastor and preacher at St Martin-in-the-Fields, London, and William Temple, this Anglican pastor sought to make the Gospel live in difficult times. He was the 12th of 14 children.

He explored the problem of suffering and obviously in a religious framework it was to ask how could an omnipotent God watch, "the beloved creation tearing itself to shreds". As Gurlong continues, "if the explanation was that God, in some way, was suffering at the hands of human hatred, then how could God be said to be omnipotent? Kennedy gave the simple soldier the dignity of straining and groping towards a recognition of God's place in the midst of suffering."

The first play, entitled *War! Lies! And A Packet of Fags* and written by David Gooderson, received a rehearsed reading at the London and International School of Acting in January 1992. A shortened version was broadcast on BBC Radio 4 under a changed title of *Waste of Glory*, and hence its place in this chapter.

The second play could well find its place in the general chapter dealing with Jesus on Stage and contemporary works, but rather than split things it seems reasonable to continue in this context. The play *Woodbine Willie* was written by David Hill and was a one-man piece, and in this case played with considerable ability by the actor Bill Wiesener who some say even looked like Kennnedy. Initially *Woodbine Willie* played at The Emery, a small East London theatre space. Hill says both he and Bill were fans of Kennedy and had a great admiration for his life.

They ran with his sense of Jesus as the man with the cap busying himself at the carpenter's bench, a man of the people. It chimes well with the words of Dick Sheppard who remarked at his death that he was, "a saint – a real saint." It meant, Gurling says, that to the poor, the workless and the old soldiers, he was one of their own.

Hill with Bill Wiesener took their play out of the East End and played a variety of locations throughout Britain, achieving over 100 performances. Hill speaks of a great reception, and encountering many who had met the very man himself. At these performances Wiesener did not give out the ciggies but produced a packet and made appropriate giving gestures. Unfortunately the text has never been published. Over a number of years these two talented individuals brought all kinds of drama to the London East End at the Emery Theatre and encouraged work to come from the community. They also bravely provided paid work to actors rather than rely on some assumed goodness from an actor who has said he or she is a Christian, and so will pass when it comes to financial reward. Unfortunately local by-laws and council interference with their licensing rules and regulations did the theatre no favours, and certainly not the people who pay their council tax.

In 1991, Radio Hallam, in a moment of sheer bravery for a commercial station, carried my play *Warning! Religion Can Damage Your Health*. It lasted 90 minutes, even more courageous for an independent station, and its radio station controller, Keith Skues. In drama terms it meant the play had the air of a soap opera, with crescendo points to the ad-breaks. It was directed by Margaret Robertson, well known as a playwright, producer and actress. Among the actors were Polly March and Anne-Lee Wakefield, known at the time for her role in the *Rocky Horror Show*. Song lyrics came from Ernest Marvin. It was about a young person finding faith, at the same time the text was asking about the nature and person of Jesus that was being offered to young people.

This text can only focus on a small number of areas and of course the BBC Religious Radio department has contributed numerous programmes in many styles and formats, not least the adventurous series *Seeds of Faith*, to which this writer contributed on a number of occasions. Sadly, and not it might be said from a personal perspective, this creative and adventurous half-hour was withdrawn from the schedules – it had difference, a time for the unexpected. In December 2007 the BBC commissioned five radio plays based on the Gospel of Luke by Nick Warburton. The series is called *Witness* and is available on CD from BBC Publications.

The calendar may change dates but in religious circles some things never go away. To take a massive leap in time is to arrive in 2006. The BBC involved itself in an alternative Passion. It achieved the togetherness of BBC2 and BBC3 TV. The initial news reports spoke of an hour long contemporary retelling of the crucifixion and resurrection. The drama was called *The Manchester Passion*. The orchestral score would involve Manchester-based songs over the past 30 years. It was suggested the character playing Jesus would regale the disciples at the Last Supper with *Joy Division's* tear-jerker, 'Love Will Tear Us Apart'. Judas would have the unutterable privilege of raiding *The Smith's* catalogue for one of Morrissey's all-time downer songs, 'Heaven knows I'm

Miserable Now'. The momentum established was good. The relocation of crucifixion and resurrection worked brilliantly, with Jesus well played by Darren Morfitt. The modern nature of the presentation was especially evident when just as Jesus declared at supper that someone present would betray him, Judas had a mobile call which summoned him to the High Priest's apartment. David Bridge of the *Methodist Recorder* notes that when under arrest Jesus appeared in a Guantanamo style orange jump suit, and he announced his resurrection from the top of the Town Hall tower. There were those who still complained. It would be disappointing if there were not.

Two years on and in 2008 the centrepiece of the BBC's Easter season was *The Passion* which gained a prime-time slot and ran over four weeks. It was co-financed with the American HBO. It is a fact of life these days that any expensive drama has to find other funders than the originator. That in itself has curtailing and negative effects for it means trying to find a common ground that may be acceptable in differing cultures and understandings, and which process can pull away from anything controversial that might hinder the financial underpinning. So in other words, an intrinsic story can be edited not on the basis of its own merit but so as not to offend any of the involved parties.

Interestingly the producer Nigel Stafford-Clark engaged the Christian community with pre-screening dialogue – that it was necessary inadvertently says something pretty dire about some sections of the Christian world in the 21st century. Perhaps. Mr Stafford-Clark was wise, and indeed one magazine supplement pointed out that when he made *Bleak House* he had to field complaints from the Dickens Society. It cannot be a very pleasant thought to have the vapid shouts from intolerant areas of presumed Christian standing coming your way!

His trenchant observation rested in saying, "My job is telling stories. The fact that it is the backbone of one of the world's great religions is what, for me, has stopped it being told properly as a story before because people back away from it." He assured readers that *The Passion* was not remotely controversial. "There is no attempt to twist anything – you don't see Jesus sleeping with Mary Magdalene or anything like that. People are looking for something beyond their new car. Telling a story like this quenches that thirst. It makes you feel there is something beyond your own limited existence."

As someone who has predominantly presented material within a church setting I can feel for what he says and his world is vastly larger than mine, yet I am always conscious that part and parcel of much drama rests in causing shock. That I have to be about moving people on.

Peter Stansford in *The Observer*, who was not writing per se to support the BBC producer, recalled how controversy has often followed adaptations of Christian material. He mentions for instance lapsed Catholic Martin Scorsese's depiction of Jesus having erotic dreams about Mary Magdalene in his 1988 movie *The Last Temptations of Christ*, with accompanying demonstrations of protest outside cinemas. In his view it is as far back as Franco Zeffirelli's 1977 mini-series *Jesus of Nazareth* where one can find a version "that pleased most of the people most of the time." He continues, "That seems to be an outcome the BBC is seeking with *The Passion*, a counterbalance, some have suggested, to the offence it caused to some churchgoers by broadcasting *Jerry Springer: The Opera* in 2005."

The script was by Frank Deasy. To many this was quite a coup, although Deasy interviewed in *The Stage* does say that he touched base with the BBC, and asked to be considered as the drama's writer.

At the time he was hot stuff. He had just finished working on the much lauded *Prime Suspect* where Helen Mirren so compellingly played Jane Tennyson, a top notch policewoman who was spiritually bereft, who was facing the end of her career and apart from her job had to deal with alcoholism. So here was a top writer working with a religious production, although at base it was a BBC drama production.

In an interview carried by *The Stage* (March 20, 2008) he reported feeling that the various religious renditions of the passion he had watched were dramatically quite lazy. He wanted to develop the characters and amongst those he had a "soft spot" for Judas. So too he wanted to gain a more human image of Mary, and so get past the image of her as the "adoring, approving mother of God."

But of course, what of Jesus? He tells *The Stage* journalist Matthew Hemley: "I was drawn to the possibility of writing a character like Jesus who is a powerhouse of spiritual strength, and the opportunity to explore that was exciting. I also like the universality of the themes in Jesus' story. It is about human frailty in the face of suffering and death, but it is also about overcoming suffering to find true love. It is very redemptive and in that way different from things I have done before." Deasy and others paid visits to the Holy Land to gain insight and which he says led him to "making the concepts Jesus talks about as simple as that." Fair enough but at the same time the Gospel narratives from day one carry the sinister tone of humankind at war with itself, so that it may no longer push goodness to the fore but be more in love with the dark side of human nature. Even, for instance, in the beauty of traditional Christmas narratives there is never absent the thought that the good shall be pushed aside in the ever present chase for power – that will in turn be misused to crush the poor.

"Whether they see Jesus as an historical figure or God, what we have tried to do is create a drama that stands on its own, so people of any and no faith can find it enjoyable." It is of course the word 'enjoyable' that sticks in the gullet. Would the distinguished writer use that word about his terrific scripts and the overall portrayals within *Prime Suspect*? If so, then all is well, if not, then it begs many questions, for at least to this writer, the gospel narratives are closer to the murky underworld of the police saga than to any sense of unquestioned well being.

Overall *The Passion* generated much interest and praise from some quarters, with reservations from others. *The Observer* gathered together a cross section of religious leaders and also added to its ecumenical list the view of Terry Sanderson, President of the National Secular Society. Sanderson said his concern was not with any theological shadings, more with whether he felt he was watching good drama, and he was not. He found the first episode baffling and confused. He felt that no-one would be attracted by the

Jesus character so that they will give Christianity another look. "He is uncharismatic and impossible to distinguish from the other apostles." Similar expression came from some of the others contributing their thoughts.

The Revd. Joanna Jepson, Vicar of St Peter's Fulham and chaplain to the London College of Fashion felt that if her non-Christians friends saw it they would not understand from this drama why Jesus is so powerful, nor the magnitude of what he did. Rabbi Julia Neuberger had mixed feelings. She felt the dialogue seemed to "pull the whole thing down into being a kind of domestic drama in a wonderful, historical setting." Maulana Shadidraza, Director of Imams' and Mosques' Council of the UK appreciated the emphasis on the humanity of Jesus while Bishop Kieran Conry was very favourable to Penelope Wilson's playing of Mary, but he says little about Jesus. His final thrust rested in congratulating the BBC in making the series possible, something he thought would not have been possible ten years previous.

David Bridge in the *Methodist Recorder* defined clearly what it was: "It is a film abut the passion story from the point of view of the people who were there." He thought it succeeded magnificently. There were minor quibbles but these were of no real importance in what was a powerful, and at times, deeply moving drama. Bridge thought everything had come a long way from the happenings surrounding and relating to *The Man Born To Be King*. He recalls The Lord's Day Observance Society complaining, "A sinful man presuming to impersonate the Sinless One, it detracts from the honour due to the Divine Majesty."

As for Jesus played by Joseph Mawle, he saw the sense of someone with a clear identity of his destiny and a special relationship with God. He was someone who would make people laugh.

Bridge found a particularly impressive moment during the crucifixion scene when Jesus, nailed to a cross, was being lifted onto the upright: The camera was so positioned that the earth moved rather than the body and we looked down on Christ from above. As in Salvador Dali's painting, 'Christ of St John of the Cross', we had God's view of the event.

The big critical 'yes' came from *The Guardian's* TV columnist in its daily supplement G2, with the lead-in caption saying: "The Easter story goes real time in the BBC's down and dirty new adaptation – and it's brilliant."

This chapter has only concerned itself with the most visible (BBC or ITV) output, and this has been a brief treatment. However it is clear that all the providers like and excel at programmes dealing with Christmas and Easter. There are of course exceptions, several of which stem from the brilliance of Norman Stone, with Jack Clemo and *Shadowlands* (based on C.S.Lewis) and *Florence Nightingale*.

Money is of course the constant dilemma. A hugely expensive production has to justify itself in terms of quality, audience appeal or attractiveness to co-funders to get commissioned and broadcast. Unlike American television there is no sense that money is the two-way traffic of the religious TV industry: money taken from viewers in the form of 'sacramental' contributions and money returned in the less tangible form of celestial jackpots, that have been described as 'Sanctimoney.' As Martin Amis once said Americans don't feel the same way about money as the British. "They are not embarrassable on the subject. Money is its own vindication; money is its own just cause." It does of course mean that this writer cannot have the pleasure of describing Jesus on stage against the background of evangelists who heal and reward over the airwaves.

CHAPTER NINE

Final Thoughts

Whatever the choice of art form, there has never been a time when portrayal of Jesus has been the subject of unanimous approach and approval. This is hardly surprising when any idea as to what Jesus may have looked or sounded like is left to the imagination. There are some supposed guides. Inferences are drawn from supposition: for instance, it is assumed that Jesus was a 'kind' person, and so a portrait artist might give Jesus a friendly face. The stage actor might take on board the likelihood that Jesus must have had a loud voice or considerable vocal projection since the scriptural record says that he stood in a boat off shore and taught those on land. For the same reason, a casting director will avoid the softly spoken actor or certainly one who has spent much time in film and television.

Astonishingly, some Christians avidly debate the question: 'Did Jesus laugh?' and if we assume that it is possible that he did, then, for the actor, there is the interesting dilemma as to the kind of laughter. Was it quiet, perhaps more of a chuckle, or at the other extreme full-throated, even a bellow? John Aldridge writing for *The Methodist Recorder* in May 2005 believes that any jokes Jesus told would be worthy, engaging and never hurtful. Indeed there is a web site devoted to the idea of Jesus laughing (www.jesuslaughing.com), but it is an aspect that is not noticeable in scripts submitted to us. Other than the earlier mentioned *Godspell* with its humour and playfulness, when it comes to major playwrights there is little laughter observed. Only in Steven Berkoff's *Messiah* do provocative theories about biblical texts mingle with laddish jokes about women and backstage lepers told by Jesus.

We have found that there is considerable ignorance on the part of some playwrights as to the ethnic origin of Jesus. One thing is certain: whatever the arguments concerning the qualities of the living Jesus, the inescapable fact is simply that he was Jewish. Fact or not, some famous and revered individuals have often preferred to portray Jesus as European and a few have considered or hoped that he was American.

Jesus' Jewish background leads to the possibility that he was probably a very fine story teller. But if the actor were to take this on board he might be tempted to adopt the distinct and persuasive style embedded in Jewish mannerisms. This simple fact is usually ignored by drama groups. Often such groups will prefer to enact the Jesus story outside of its immediate context and time, and so play with ideas of how he might come across if his background had not been carpentry with his father Joseph, but, say, the son of an English, West Country farmer.

We saw a production based on the story of the prodigal son. The writer was keen to show the folly of the son and the joy of the father when the son came home after his ill-adventures in a distant country. The actual play and music were enjoyable, but the writer did not seem to be aware that every reference in the story has distinct meanings within a Jewish context. In fact, the substance of this story would have angered many of its original listeners. The son continually breaks Jewish tradition, and for much of the audience, deserved a 'right telling off' rather than eventually being treated like royalty. The father goes overboard to express forgiveness and inner joy. The story would have divided the audience.

We do not accept that playwrights or theatre companies should ignore the Jewishness of Jesus simply because it may offend some Jewish people or because they are uncertain as to how a non-Jewish audience might respond. An enormous amount of scholarly literature has debated the issue of how it was that Jesus lived totally within Judaism, and yet was the origin of a movement that eventually separated from Judaism.

We do see that Jewish humour is considerably different from Christian, and this is one of themes that can be found in the book *From Faith to Fun: The Secularization of Humour* by Russell Heddedorf. A book such as *Jesus and Judaism* by E.P. Sanders should be mandatory reading for playwright, director and actor when the basic narratives of Scripture are dramatised. In terms of its overall claims, more questionable and debatable is *The Changing Faces of Jesus* by Geza Vermes (note also his earlier *Jesus the Jew*). In the early 1940s Laurence Housman achieved some attention for what were termed the 'Palestine Plays'. Woven in amongst his declared writing intention, Housman desired to rid the Old Testament of "useless excrescences."

The Jewish aspect has been very much in the mind of Christian Stueckl, the director of the 2010 re-enactment of the *Crucifixion at Oberammergau* where two actors were cast in the role of Jesus. Stueckl told *The Times,* January 30, 2010, "We have to present the historical Jesus even if we know only a few things for sure about him. As a Jesus who can only be understood with reference to his Jewish faith. That's how we want to do it this year – to depict Jesus who fights with unbelievable determination to stay true to his God, who is also the God of Abraham, the God of Isaac, in other words, the God of the Jews." Post-war productions have been overshadowed by accusations of anti-Semitism, and in 1977 the production was avoided by Jewish organisations. The 2010 enactment sees among numerous changes the deletion of the line, "His blood is upon us and upon our children's children." At the Last Supper, Jesus says the blessing in Hebrew. It has to be remembered that Adolph Hitler attended a performance in 1934 and is reported as saying, "It is of importance to the Reich." Save for Judas, all cast members were pro-Nazi.

In our reading of 'church plays', we find that too few playwrights have contemplated the inescapable fact that the life of Jesus must be understood in the context of Jewish society and belief. We do not see this as deliberate. In practical terms, however, it presents an intriguing dilemma, for does a Christian church that wishes to have someone play the person of Jesus genuinely search for a Jewish actor who would have no qualms in enacting the role? But where does this leave the imaginations of the actor and his audience?

There are of course even deeper questions. How, for example, does an actor engage in his approach to performance with such concepts as 'Jesus the Messiah,' or 'Jesus, the Son of God?' The average church- written play so often simply gives the character words straight from the Gospels. The creation of 'character' requires the provision of dialogue, action, interaction, motivation and context. An actor's preparation and research must explore all these elements of drama.

Walt Kissack played Jesus in the Riding Lights Company presentation of *Redemption Song*. He recalls that one man was outraged by the human portrayal of Jesus and vented his anger towards the liberal agenda he felt was being imposed. It seems people were either moved or incensed by the drama. The actor says, "When trying to interpret and understand someone else's experience as set out in a script, my first point of reference has to be my own experience, or my own understanding of someone else's experience. In terms of understanding the nature of Jesus my first concern was that his couldn't be any further away from my own."

For Lee Rhodes, who once took the lead in *Jesus Christ Superstar*, all was not well, At the end of July 2009, the *Camden New Journal*, London, reported an inquest on his death. His body was found by a dog walker in the bushes near Whitestone pond in May. A friend and theatre-land impresario, Kevin Wallace, said that the 38 year-old actor didn't just play Jesus but really, "became the role in a unique transformation on stage." It was said that he over-identified with the lead role and expressed feelings of guilt that he could not, "help or heal on the street in the way the character he was playing could." In a wonderful piece of satire carried by an American publication *Pews News* it was reported that Pastor John Truefaith was found dead on a cross by a cleanup crew the following morning at Landover Baptist's Platinum Christian Coliseum. It appeared that in scene 32 the Roman actors became so immersed in their characters that they actually killed Jesus. A comment later said: "This is the first year our actors tried 'The Method' and we'll revisit that decision if it will save lives."

Other than the occasional reference, we have not discussed in this book the portrayal of Jesus in art, or opera, in classical music oratorios, or poetry, novel and film, but we make one other reference beyond our strict brief – after all, even in Latin there are exceptions. In 2004 the Tate Britain exhibition gave us a somewhat provocative piece of work from Sarah Lucas, *Christ You Know It Ain't Easy*. The Crucifixion was made up of discarded 'Marlboro Light ciggies'.

There was little comment from the Church, and the same was true of Damien Hirst's take on the Passion; a cow carcass entitled *The Pursuit of Oblivion*. As Michael Gove wrote in *The Times* (December 14, 2004) the only objection emanated from the Evangelical Alliance at Hirst's depiction of Jesus lying in a cardboard box marked 'Quality Office Products', and the title he gave his work, *Jesus is Laid in the Tomb*.

For Christmas in the same year, Madame Tussauds decided to depict David and Victoria Beckham as Mary and Joseph with Tony Blair, George Bush and the Duke of Edinburgh as The Three Wise Men, and Samuel L. Jackson, Hugh Grant and Graham Norton as shepherds. Kylie Minogue was an angel. But there was no Jesus. Perhaps fortunately. That said, *The Times* ran with the headline "Remember Jesus? He's that baby they all forgot in the parable of Tussauds." *The Times* writer Michael Gove believes, "we have become inured towards all this hostility directed at Christianity." Should our text have achieved anything it may rest on our having displayed the plethora of dramatic material that deals with the figure of Jesus.

During our study we have, of course, passed comment in the light of our theological and religious nuances, and doubtless prejudices, but it is not possible to state unequivocally what is an effective or truthful portrayal of Jesus in each and every situation. Equally we cannot be the judge of what might be deemed orthodox or heretical. We have our opinions. We have suggested strongly that orthodoxy and heresy may not belong to their supposed traditional masters. Some church-based production texts have been found to innocently espouse deviant tendencies.

We have clearly shown that those outside official Christian circles often produce penetrating and exciting insights into Christian truth. Some within are so cabined, cribbed and confined by the pressures of what they feel they ought to say, that their work is static and uninteresting. We have seen that in recent times writers such as Howard Brenton, John Patrick Shanley, Stephen Adly Guirgis, Roger Crane, David Hare, and Steven Berkoff have explored aspects of the Christian faith without the permission of Methodists in their offices in London's Marylebone Road, the blessing of Anglicans at Church House, the support of the United Reformed Church in Tavistock Square or the approval of Baptists in Didcot. Their plays have occasioned much thought and debate. We are not aware of churches organising coach trips to watch their plays as they did for productions of *Godspell*, *Jesus Christ Superstar*, and more recently Mel Gibson's limited and literalist film *The Passion of the Christ*.

This is a depressing state of affairs for it would seem that some Christians only wish to see a portrayal of Jesus that fits in with their scheme of things, or perhaps might lead the invited 'outsider' to contemplate what is often termed 'coming to Christ.' However, there is admittedly a difficulty in deciding what might be termed mainstream or orthodox belief. When it comes to groups whose theology veers in often a narrow and more fundamentalist direction, it becomes one of life's mysteries as to why groups from Pentecostalist or independent church backgrounds should see faith salvation in either the Gibson screenplay or the text of Webber-Rice's *Superstar*.

It is obvious that the Jesus of the media has been claimed and shaped for desired effect, sometimes to give credence to other systems deemed more worthy. Those ever searching for their own relevance, and perhaps finding themselves unwanted and unloved by the church youth group may, for example, suddenly decide that Jesus was hip and not square, that he would have rapped his message and not been given over to parables. Perhaps the 21st century Jesus would have found the recording star Eminem a likely friend in communication styles but that in itself would have been a natural process. By way of contrast, we have often found in church based plays a disquieting element of trying to find ways into the cultural forms of the moment. Rarely does such a process succeed. For a play text to make sense it must come from *within* the culture so that it becomes a natural product. Perhaps the best example of this is the earlier mentioned *A Man Dies*. We are not attempting to decry amateur productions and we are not saying that all church produced work is uninspired – far from it.

We are interested in raising standards and we would say this to any writer, director, actor, choreographer or designer, whether paid or unpaid.

Words must endure misrepresentation. Take for instance the term "Quaker". In the 17th century this word became a convenient label for any unconventional religionist, and many things were doubtless laid at the door of the Quakers which belonged to other sects. In the same way at particular moments in history the word 'theatre' has been for some Christian people a dirty word as though involving a degree of dishonesty. We have been aware in assembling our text and talking with many, that drama where Jesus is an actual character, rather than someone referred to, can be seen as blasphemous. No such compulsion applies to demons and the Devil. Through the centuries demons in pictorial and dramatic representation wore hideous masks with horns and a tail. We might misquote General Booth and ask 'why should the Devil have all the best parts?'

We have seen how society has used its voice in determining what is and what is not acceptable in drama when given a 'religious coating'. Not so long ago Lord Reith of the BBC opposed religious broadcasting on national radio because it might be heard by men in public houses who would not be wearing hats. Many indignant reactions accompanied the war-time radio broadcast of Dorothy L. Sayers's *The Man Born to be King*. Parliament discussed whether an early '60s TV production of *A Man Dies* constituted blasphemy in suggesting that Mary the harlot had sexual thoughts about Jesus and that he might have had a mild interest in this testy young woman.

As we have shown there has always been a 'Christian voice' of sorts ready to pronounce from outside the profes-

sional circles of clergy. Certainly a vociferous lobby of agita-
tors is easily assembled and in recent times a chosen object
of noisy distaste was the American production of *Jerry
Springer: The Opera*. Some suggest the 'shouters' were blind
to what the production was actually saying. The show was in
fact a vicious attack on the 'selling' of religion, and of situations where ministry has been superseded by business. This
message has escaped many who claim to be Christians and
yet seem totally unaware of the major scandals that have
erupted in various evangelical wings of the Church both in
Britain and the United States. William Drew counters such
myopic vision in the magazine *Interact*, July, 2006, when he
says: "Though it may seem that blasphemy is de rigueur on
the British stage today, the theatre is an ideal location for
issues of faith to be addressed."

We cannot escape the conclusion that for some 'religious'
people drama is but a tool, and a minor one at that, in telling
the Christian story. It would be considered a major tool if it
produced results, but to many, it seems to be a rather long
and involved form. They desire something uncomplicated
where what they deem to be the message is spoken plain and
clear. Should it be both those things and prayed about hard
enough beforehand, then converts will be made, or at least
that seems to be the simple thought process for desired
success.

There is further a desire to present only the defined
'good' and so there is no place for assuming any of the disciples ever uttered an unholy thought. This carries into
general character writing where the defined Christian is
always seen as patient, worthy, loving, and so one could
continue a list of pleasant words! There is the extraordinary
thought that non-Christians in the audience watching a
'Christian' play must only see a 'Christian' character who
says and does no wrong, and in lifestyle has no contradic-
tions. For the writer the 'Christian' person has arrived at
some kind of pristine state. Hence a degree of anguish from
'Christian' quarters should a character be described as
pregnant outside of marriage, or utters profanities. It leads
to an insert in the programme notice, "In this play the character Tessa is described as a Christian. However, she is also

seen as pregnant and outside of marriage. The church wishes it to be known that this is only true of a handful of such believers. It is the teaching of...."

In such circles drama becomes more favoured as some kind of link item in a so-called modern worship service and thus more often than not the quick sketch or brief re-enactment of a biblical story. There is little attempt to get behind the narrative, or to understand why it might have found its way into the respective Gospel. In reality this is no more than an attempt to dress up a particular scriptural translation with something that is instant and ear-catching so that the chosen passage is *heard*. It is quite another matter as to whether it is digested or makes sense and usually that level of insight is not seen as terribly important in the overall scheme of things. Much of this rather laboured process might have some value if greater attention was given to the use of the voice, the use of microphone, breath control and physical poise and, above all, a search for truth.

Even the simple process of reading a church lesson would benefit from the insights of drama and performance. Readers, quite apart from speaking too rapidly or quietly, or adopting a clerical whine, lack the actor's sense of the passage that is theirs to read. In our experience the 'well sent ahead' lesson information remains dormant until some minutes before a service and there is rarely evidence of that level of preparation quintessential to an actor's craft. Perhaps it is little wonder that lessons are read badly and lack the freshness that demands the attention of the listeners as if they were hearing those words for the first time. As one great theatre director remarked during rehearsal of some complex text, "It must be born afresh in you every day." We have yet to meet a chapel steward or lesson reader who articulates the desire to capture the offensiveness of the Gospel in its own time. Even theological colleges report a resistance of would-be ministers to face their limitations as readers of the Word. It is no co-incidence that cathedrals, colleges and Rabbis are turning to actors as mentors in this important aspect of their work. The theatre director Declan Donellan says in his usual pithy way: "If we never dare explore the rim of our capacities, we can never expand them."

The concepts and practice of drama itself change and are constantly seen in different lights by their practitioners. This also has an effect on how Jesus is perceived and indeed enacted in a stage production. In general stage theatre, as opposed to television drama, there is little fear these days about taking Jesus to the stage and it is considered to be of little relevance if such portrayal is uncomfortable and unsettling for audiences. Nor is an actor playing the role of Jesus encouraged or expected to be more superficially 'holy' and upstanding than the average person.

As we have shown Christians may have ignored the theatre but the theatre has not ignored Jesus. In fact, he is the most represented historical figure in modern drama. In theatre, if not in the churches, Jesus is alive!

The world today needs a theatre that shows people how they might act constructively. Harold Hobson wrote in the *Sunday Times* 1964 that the time had come to move on. He noted that the texts of the time expressed disillusionment, protest and denunciation, and that although this could be positive when directed against corruption and hypocrisy he felt the need for assertion.

Yet nearly 50 years later the same language is heard. The July 2009 Independent Theatre Council Summer Conference had as its theme 'Facing and Forging the Future'. Those attending were assaulted by a brilliant speaker Stewart Wallis of the New Economics Foundation. He outlined planetary perils far in excess of those conjured up in the hey-day by the Westminster Theatre and Moral Rearmament when many a production was concerned with the inhumanities of humanism and the callousness of a permissive morality. Through this, and similar thoughts expressed by others, ITC asked people how they would see a resilient and relevant future for the arts. Discussion verged on the very areas that religion sometimes claims for its own, the nature of society, the citizen, the issue of participation. Not surprisingly delegates went on to suggest the importance of theatre in educating and questioning a whole range of pressing issues. Theatre practitioners were disturbed that it was hard to exist as a company or artist, and more so because their work and method was under-valued.

At the end of that same week there was Nicholas Hytner, the artistic director of the prestigious Royal National Theatre, London, in the *Financial Times*, July 18/19, 2009, keen to be seen as someone who commissions work that grapples with the biggest issues of the day, events that seem so significant that they must be addressed. David Hare, whose plays and speeches have challenged almost every aspect of Christian belief is one such commissioned writer. In directing his play *The Power of Yes* Hytner tells of his objectives to the feature writer Sarah Hemming: "It represents part of the National's role as a civic forum...It is a good thing for a national theatre to be involved in explanation, investigation and the provocation of strong emotional and intellectual response to the world around us. If we provoke outrage, justifiably, that's good. And if we find more nuances in something that has been treated as a story with a very clear set of villains, that would be good too."

The esteemed director goes on to say, "a lot of theatres are confident about their part in the national conversation and they have enthusiastic audiences that want to be part of this kind of debate."

But, at the same time, there is the dear old Church speaking to no-one but itself and relegating drama to the 'be considered, but take no further action' pile. Its Scriptures are loaded with references to faith and community, but its own practice and exploration of such is left to the few while in the main it marches serenely to its death. Sadly we do not find the power structures of the Church particularly receptive to the potential of theatre and drama.

There was a time when particular churches had their own arts and drama advisors but little of this impetus and encouragement remains. We ask why the Christian Church annually spends millions of pounds on music yet does not even have a budget for drama. We take one example: The Diocese of Canterbury has no budget for anyone who bears the title of Drama Adviser. This is a Cathedral that maintains a choir, a school and several full-time appointments in music, not to mention possessing one of the largest organs in the world! The British Methodist Church once far seeing and generous in supporting the Arts relies on volunteers.

We are aware of scrambling small theatre companies that explore religious themes and with considerable impact when they can afford to function, and whose work gains little financial support from churches that often cry they have no money. These Christian concerns at the same time spend vast sums on other sometimes questionable activities.

Naturally, it will be said by our opponents that there are many things upon which the Church can spend its money and resources. The Church, like a Government, must choose and some areas will unfortunately suffer. Naturally, in better times, these 'minor' areas can receive attention. That is no more than a cop-out for it neither names what is essential nor has the courage (vision?) to say that any decision is built upon certain assumptions.

We do not support the apparent decision of the churches to relegate consideration of drama to an after-thought. We believe the Church should be engaging the minds of people, and drama rates highly on that score. We totally reject the concept of drama as something merely useful to young people, or something pleasant to engage all age-groups, or a form of entertainment per se. We believe the Church should be quick to respond to crucial world and local events, and where it is situated on major public thoroughfares it should be offering commentary from the perspectives of Faith. We call on the respective churches to establish drama practitioners and centres that offer daily and weekly input and indeed at the same time input into worship – worship of such quality that it makes special the whole of life, for we suggest we need to recover a wholeness in all our living.

We are mindful that amidst the abject failures of most Church structures much is owed to the likes of Paul Burbridge (Riding Lights), the Gibbs Trust, and broadcaster-actor-director-writer Nigel Forde, whose inspirational thoughts can be found in his book *TheatreCraft*. The Arts Centre Group has from time to time sponsored drama deriving much of its drive in theatrical terms from Nigel Goodwin. Goodwin's London 'pad' in Knightsbridge was the place where a number of actors made their way after nightly shows to enjoy company, food, prayer and perhaps a little commiseration if the audiences were not packing the seats of their production. Methodists have owed much to Rachel Newton and Peter Moreton. The Arts Centre Group varies its membership but in 1999/2000 it listed 107 working actors who obviously had a Jesus connection! In recent time the ACG has experienced a fresh surge of life.

We believe in the theatre and the arts. We believe in them passionately. We believe that for many people they are the means above all other whereby the spirit of God can be communicated to them. But that is why we also believe that the arts should be taken seriously, studied, worked at and respected.

Christians of all shades of expression should find consolation that the person of Jesus still invites writing from some of the best dramatists, and that at the same time there has been a marked revival in the presentation of the 'Mystery' plays. We have devoted considerable space in this book to the revival of ancient plays dealing with the life of Jesus and with the significance of His coming to earth as part of a divine plan. The various hostilities and social conditions that had led to the neglect of the Mystery Plays and of the Passions in particular have largely, although not entirely disappeared and, especially during the last twenty years, there have been numerous highly effective productions in which the figure of Jesus has been central. However, even though the presentation of such plays has been eagerly espoused by various Christian groups and individuals, they have often been less a means of evangelism and more an exercise in social cohesion.

Rather than being a celebration of common belief many Mystery Plays projects have been celebrations of common values. The Cornish plays have been identified with a resurgence of Cornish nationalism and the plays associated with British cities have, to some extent, been seen both as a Christian witness and as artistic treasures, like the cathedrals that have sustained them. In the hands of the Royal Shakespeare Company or the Royal National Theatre, the Mystery Plays have shown Jesus as a dynamic figure far removed from the Sunday School or children's illustrated Bible image and it was fascinating to hear a modern Christian director maintaining that it had been necessary to find a non-Christian playwright to create a script for a Passion Play that was seen as relevant to the contemporary world. A Jesus overlaid with piety and sentimentality, speaking the words of the Authorised Version of the Bible can be insufferably cloying, reducing drama to the level of a comfort blanket. The best productions of the Mystery Plays have shown that to be misguided and counter-productive for those who care about the faith and the theatre.

There has even been an unexpected export of an Easter Mystery Play which started life on the streets of Edinburgh, and has now been performed in Uganda, and is set to spread further around East Africa. Although the original English script was used as a basis, actors performed the drama in their local language.

Various individuals have been praised for their efforts, and we have in our view been justified in castigating mainstream churches for their almost total lack of tangible support. We cannot end without uttering massive praise to Peter Hutley and his wife Ann, who transform their 1,000 acre Wintershall Estate in Surrey each year into a first century Palestine to stage *The Life of Christ* featuring 207 actors, 30 sheep, 15 horses, two donkeys and a camel. The only paid member of the cast is Jesus who has been played with some style in recent years by James Burke Dunsmore. The production regularly attracts audiences of 3000. The director Ashley Herman was approached by Hutley while he was working in the London West End theatre with Lily Savage in *Prisoner Cell Block H*. Herman is reported as saying that for him *The Life Of Christ* is "about the transcendental power of theatre."

At least in theatre and in the streets Jesus is far from dead.

This a wake-up call to churches. We need to put Jesus centre stage.

Bibliography

Anon, ed. Kemp E with Mitchell, K. (1997) *The Mysteries*, London: Nick Hern.

Bradley, I. (2004) *You've Got To Have A Dream*, London: SCM.

Braun, M. (1972) *Jesus Christ Superstar. The Authorized Version*, London: Pan.

Browne, H and E.M, (1945) *Pilgrim Story*, London: Frederick Muller.

Buckner, R. (1993) *The Joy of Jesus - Humour in the Gospels*, Norwich: Canterbury Press.

Clarke-Smith, S. (1901) *The Miracle Play in England*, London: William Andrews.

Dewar, L. (1949) *New Testament Ethics*, London: University of London Press.

Eversole, F. ed. (1962) *Christian Faith and the Contemporary Arts*, NY: Abingdon.

Forde, N. (1986). *Theatrecraft*, London: Marc Europe.

Heddendorf, R. (2009) *From Faith to Fun - The Secularization of Humour*, London: Lutterworth.

Honeycombe, G. (1964) *The Redemption*, London: Methuen.

Hussey, M. (1957) *The Chester Mystery Plays* , London: Heinemann.

Jasper, T. (1974) *Jesus in a Pop Culture*, London: Collins.

Johnson T. E. Savidge D. (2009) *Performing the Sacred: Theology and Theatre in Dialogue*, Baker Academic.

Martin, Malachi (1975) *Jesus Now*, London: Collins.

Miles, K. (1981) *Coventry Mystery Plays*, London: Heinemann.

Moynahan, M.E. (1998) *Once upon a Mystery*, New York: Paulist Press.

O' Leary, D.J. and Sallnow, T. (1982) *Love and Meaning in Religious Education - The Incarnational Approach to Teaching Christianity*, Oxford: OUP.

Pickering, K. (2001) *Drama in the Cathedral*, Colwall: Garnet Miller.

Purvis, Rev. J.S. (1953) *The York Cycle of Mystery Plays*, London: SPCK.

Sanders, E.P. (1985) *Jesus and Judaism*, London: SCM.

Sugano, D and Pickering, K. (1997) *The Midlands' Mysteries*, Colwall: Garnet Miller.

Taylor, T. (1916) *The Celtic Christianity of Cornwall*, London: Longman, Green & Co.

Tillich, P. (1955) *The New Being*, London: SCM.

Vermes, Geza (2000) *The Changing Face of Jesus*, Harmonsdworth: Penguin.

Wolfe, K. (1984) *The Churches and the British Broadcasting Corporation 1922-1956*, London: SCM.

Wood, D. (ed .) (1992) *The Church and the Arts*. Volume 28, London: Blackwell.

Wright, S. (2008) *The Sounds of the Sixties*, NY: Grosvenor House.

People and places

Index of Works, ordered by title

Index of Works, ordered by creators

– A –

– B –

– C –

ALSO FROM HIGHLAND BOOKS

NEXT WE SHALL SING

by
Tony Jasper

"Can't get no satisfaction" from hymns and songs? It's nigh impossible to please everyone these days, but Tony Jasper sets out to track down songs that mirror the endless pressure of God through people and situations…

- How to make the most of traditional hymns and tunes
- Trends in modern music that are more satisfying than choruses
- What to do about the surfeit of hapless material for children

"Hymnological applecarts upset like moneychangers' tables"
John Marsh, Moderator, URC Great Britain.

ISBN 978-1897913-82-6   RRP 9.99